THE CINEMA OF
DAVID LEAN

ALSO BY GERALD PRATLEY

The Cinema of John Frankenheimer
The Cinema of Otto Preminger
The Cinema of John Huston (in preparation)

THE CINEMA OF
DAVID LEAN

BY GERALD PRATLEY

PROPERTY OF
CLACKAMAS COMMUNITY COLLEGE
LIBRARY
WITHDRAWN

South Brunswick and New York: A. S. Barnes and Company
London: The Tantivy Press

PN
1998
.A3
L38
P7

© 1974 by Gerald Pratley

A. S. Barnes & Co., Inc.
Cranbury,
New Jersey 08512

The Tantivy Press
108 New Bond Street
London W1Y OQX,
England

Library of Congress Cataloging in Publication Data

Pratley, Gerald.
    The cinema of David Lean.

    1. Lean, David, 1908–   I. Title.
PN1998.A3L38   791.43′0233′0924   72-6372
ISBN 0-498-01050-3 (U. S. A.)
SBN 900 73068 4 (U.K.)
Jacket design by Stefan Dreja

Printed in the United States of America

Contents

43123

Acknowledgements

Mr. Lean's comments are drawn from interviews with the author and from material provided by the BBC, CBC, the Rank Organisation, Columbia Pictures and M-G-M. To them, and to the British Film Institute, the author extends his most grateful acknowledgements.

"I love making motion pictures. Working on the script is important and very necessary, but I'm not a word man, I'm a picture man. I love getting behind a camera and trying to get images on the screen. I love cutting and editing. I love putting all the parts together at the end: the sounds, the music, the dialogue. Making a movie is the greatest excitement of my life. Afterwards, I like taking long holidays, to find the next film, and that's always difficult. I've had some marvellous times in my life, so I tend to put some of the wonderful aspects of life on the screen. If I'm a romantic, I can only say it's because I enjoy life. I love life and I don't want to die. I want to go on making movies."

DAVID LEAN
CBC, Toronto
December, 1970
(recorded in New York)

THE CINEMA OF
DAVID LEAN

History and Appreciation

DAVID LEAN has consistently and inventively created some of the most beautiful and memorable films in the history of the cinema. He has a long record of supremely intelligent work, of entertaining in the grand manner, yet with observations that are intimate and revealing. A romantic in all respects, he is to the cinema what Dickens is to literature, Gainsborough to painting and Vaughan Williams to music. He has understood what cinema is more clearly than most other film-makers, and has shown this understanding in his visual expression of ideas, in the poetry, drama and lyricism of his images, and in his skill in adaptation, narrative form and editing technique.

In devising movements for his actors and the camera, whether for solitary figures or the massed screen, and in his feeling for landscape and atmosphere, he achieves a fine balance between pictorial composition, sound and silence, and conflicts of character and events. Throughout his work there is an unfailing concern for humanity. He understands all his characters and presents them with dignity and good taste, even if they are unkindly or cruel. His awareness of feminine psychology is deep and intuitive and in the exploration of the pleasure, passions and despair of human feeling, the cinema has few dramatists more discerning than Lean.

He is undoubtedly one of the few most powerful directors at work today; yet hardly anyone sees him or knows him. Of the many stories told about his shy and retiring nature the best is probably the one about a London correspondent assigned to write an article about David Lean, who came back to her office and reported: "David Lean, with his coal-black hair, lean face, straight, neat nose and piercing eyes, is a strikingly good-looking man. Seen in a crowd or at the studio by a stranger, he is immediately taken for an actor. Five minutes of fruitless attempts to get him to talk about himself or his work convinces you, without a shadow of a doubt, that he is not." "David's only really passionate interest in life," says Anthony Havelock-Allan, "is films. When he's making a film he's blind and deaf to everything else in the world. He'll sit at lunch and never utter a word. He has no small talk at any time and is terrifically difficult to get to know."

Directors should be as strong as iron. Lean is one of the strongest, he had to be to survive, and he realised this during the first days of filming *In Which We Serve*. Noël Coward and his officers were on the bridge of the destroyer. The set was being rocked against the back projection of the sea. The dialogue was spoken, the scene finished. "Hold your positions please," requested Lean. Coward didn't think it was necessary and he and the other actors left. The then uncertain Lean was faced with a challenge to his authority as the director. If he let the matter pass, who would respect and listen to him later? He made up his mind and sent the assistant director to bring Noël Coward and the actors back to the set. They came; Lean told them that if he asked for them to hold their positions while he checked camera and sound they would do so. Coward apologised and agreed. From that day on, David Lean has exercised complete control; but that night he told a friend who lived close to him at Denham, not far from the famous studio, that what he had done (remembering that Coward was in command) "was the gamble of my life."

★　　★　　★

Like most great artists, David Lean never talks about art, and certainly not within the context of his own achievements. He seldom talks at all except to his closest friends, who are few in number, and even then it is seldom about his work, his creativity, his ideas or ambitions. There is nothing enigmatic about his work, but he himself is something of a mystery. Since he is so unpretentious, so uncommunicative as an individual, so hesitant about going into details about himself and his films, those critics and journalists who would like to interview him or get to know him have been forced to seek information about him elsewhere, usually from actors and technicians who have worked with him. Few other directors have been described through the eyes of others to such an extent as David Lean. However, this is not always a reliable source. Most actors and craftsmen want to work with directors again and do not want to run the risk of not being employed as a result of inadvertently saying something uncomplimentary, or by being misquoted in the press. But David Lean's associates of many years standing, whose greatness as actors and technicians Lean would always value, and who are old enough and sufficiently well established to say what they please, can be depended on to give honest and direct opinions.

Trevor Howard said of Lean during the filming of *Ryan's Daughter* (their third film together), "He's really only in love with celluloid and his movieola. He doesn't really like actors. All he wants to do is get rid of them and start cutting them out of the picture. He's totally in love with film more than any other director I know."

John Mills, working for the fifth time with Lean on *Ryan's Daughter*, said, "The difference in David since *Hobson's Choice* is

Lean surveys the desert during the shooting of
LAWRENCE OF ARABIA.

staggering. He still has his fantastic technique but he's added to that a tremendous sensitivity and feeling for actors. But above all he really loves film, and to see him at work in the cutting room running it through his hands is like watching a master painter at work. The change which comes over David in the cutting room is quite remarkable."

Alec Guinness, who has, like John Mills, appeared in five of Lean's films, said of the director during the filming of *Doctor Zhivago,* that "he's easily the most meticulous artist in motion pictures, the most painstaking in every department."

Setting up a shot for BRIDGE ON THE RIVER KWAI.

These are accurate observations and a concise summing up of one of the world's few great film-makers. David Lean is far above most of his contemporaries; brilliant in what he has done and continues to do, completely without perversity and peculiarities in his style and expression, he stands largely alone, at times critically unappreciated (as most true artists are in their own time), but with the satisfaction of knowing that his films find audiences of millions around the world—particularly for *Great Expectations, Bridge on the River Kwai, Doctor Zhivago,* and lately, *Ryan's Daughter.* Of his fifteen films, which appear regularly on television in North America if not in cinemas, possibly only *Madeleine* and *The Passionate Friends* have fallen into obscurity, not because they were artistic failures, but due largely to the vagaries of distribution in which a film is never given a second chance if it fails to find an audience during initial showings. (*Oliver Twist* is seldom shown due to the controversy over the depiction of Fagin.) Lean's last four productions have earned some $213 million internationally.

★   ★   ★

David Lean began directing in wartime London, in 1942 with *In Which We Serve* with Noël Coward. Twenty-eight years later, in 1970, he completed his fifteenth film, *Ryan's Daughter*—and that was only his fourth picture made in the intervening fifteen years since finishing *Summertime,* the remaining ten having been made during the previous thirteen year period. Compared to some film-makers, his total is low. Yet Lean has never been without work, and has in fact worked consistently over this entire period, if not actually filming, preparing his next picture, reading, writing, researching, studying the subject, its people, the characters, the sociology of the structural elements, together with the all important matter of "internal faithfulness" to his source material, whether it be a book, play or original screenplay. Above all this, and most important to him, is seeing visually in his cinema mind the whole picture in the form of individual shots and sequences as they will be on the strip of film which one day will be the finished project.

"I think slowly," he says, "and there is nothing unusual about my methods. I envy people who receive sudden flashes of genius, because I don't. I try to work out every possible way to do a scene, and then choose the way that will surprise audiences. I live with my scripts, I live with my characters, and if I seem to be in another world when friends and unit people speak to me, it's because I don't have the scene solved yet. I'm frequently thought to be rude when I'm really in a mental turmoil, struggling with some problem that seems insuperable at the moment."

His cinematographer, Freddie Young, calls these moments "the David Lean stare. It's a very intense stare, and some people cannot cope with it. In some ways he's like an actor, working up to a very high pitch. Speak to him in the middle of this period of concentration and you will get the 'stare.'"

As a result of this painstaking care, David Lean has earned a reputation which emphasises his patience and quiet tenacity. He

David Lean and Sam Spiegel confer.

is devoted to his films during production. "I am told," he says rue-
fully, "that some people say I have celluloid instead of blood in
my veins. Well, I simply cannot help it. That's the way I feel
about the cinema." His methods naturally make him an easy tar-
get for critics, few of whom he particularly likes or admires. The
time and money he spends on a picture is often used against him
with such comments as "it wasn't worth it." Had they not been
told by the publicity machine how long the film was in production
and what the budget was, they might judge the picture by what
was on the screen rather than by its logistics. What they often
forget is that an artist who has proved his artistry is entitled to
attempt perfection as he sees it. In motion pictures this is extremely
difficult because of the high costs involved. Lean is one of the very
few directors to have achieved for himself the enviable but nerve-
wracking position of being given the time he needs to make a film—
a position which takes years to attain and is promptly lost just as
soon as a director with this freedom makes a film that does not
find a public large enough to bring in sufficient admission money
to cover the film's expenses.

Lean then, is usually described as "a superior craftsman" or "a brilliant technician." Just as some critics used to speak of "the Lubitsch touch" so today they speak of "the Lean technique." His insistence on trying to achieve what is for him perfection is largely responsible for this, but it denies him credit as an artist. What he possesses is a quality rare in most directors and which is best called "a film sense," but describing it is difficult. It has to be felt while watching movies, and too many critics seem to be incapable of recognising it as they have little real love for the cinema. It is an intensity of feeling which is so strong in visual and human terms that it makes the screen come to life. This has very little to do with movement either by the camera or by actors. In the case of David Lean it seems that his total obsession with film burns itself, through his visual composition and his actors, on the raw stock as it turns

David Lean directs Alec Guinness as Prince Feisal on the set of LAWRENCE OF ARABIA.

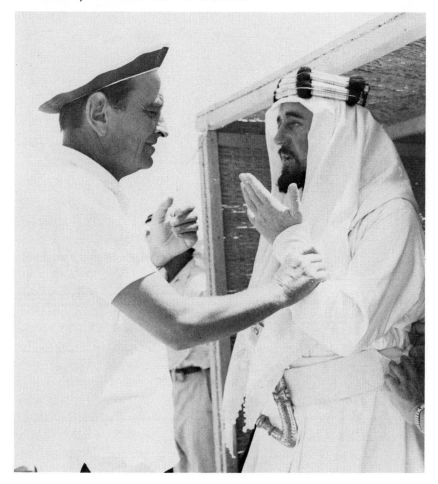

in the camera, in much the same way as a writer's passion flows into words and a painter's intensity goes into his colours and brush strokes. Anyone watching Lean direct feels this must be true in view of his complete detachment from everything going on around him and his concentration on the scene being filmed.

Often mistaken for an actor, Lean is a tall, striking, handsome man with a hawklike profile, whose sensitive, heavy-browed eyes miss nothing. He admits that he looks at everything as though he were framing it through a view-finder of a camera. He starts each working day slowly, becomes more intense and involved as the day

Lean looks on as Christopher Jones mounts up on location for RYAN'S DAUGHTER.

proceeds, often continuing late into the night without experiencing the satisfaction of obtaining in the day's filming the results he had imagined. On those days when he has succeeded, he feels a rare elation, although he also says that it's not in the day's rushes that he finds satisfaction but in the final editing. What he sees in the rushes which pleases him are the possibilities for triumphant real-isation in the editing of the whole. During this time he is a dark, brooding, thoughtful figure. The assistant directors give the orders, no one reaches Lean except his immediate associates, Freddie Young and art director, John Box, and nothing is permitted to distract him from his concentration. The script is always at hand, changed and marked by his notes and ideas. Yet he is not unfriendly, he dominates and exerts discipline over the unit, he directs forcefully and compellingly and yet in an unobtrusive way. His knowledge of technique, his gift for story-telling, his own understanding of human emotions which reach out to audiences through his actors and the events in the life of the characters they portray, his dedication and professionalism, have made him a master film-maker, totally devoid of any false mystique or image.

"People talk about what I have to say, and they tell me that I am not a personal film-maker. I don't know what they mean by this. Everything goes through me from script to final print, and nothing is done which is not a part of me. What is there to say about the human condition which hasn't been said already? The term 'originality' is used a lot, but as film-makers we can only try to be original in our depiction of themes and situations which have been known to mankind for centuries. This is really what art is all about and what people want to see. Nearly everything described as original in the cinema today is totally meaningless. It must be remembered that we are working in an expensive medium. Much of what we do must have some previous relationship with our future audience, either through a book, a play, or an event in history or present-day life.

"I'm putting into pictures something that's already there, something that has already been said perhaps, something I agree with and feel concerned about and want to make available to audiences in a visual form. Above all, I like a good story. Sometimes we take chances as with *Ryan's Daughter*, which is an original screenplay. But this does not bring a film-maker recognition as an artist. I came up through the ranks of the technicians, and for this reason no doubt, many critics continue to call me a technician, although my training was the most valuable kind. I won't call myself a writer, but I have written screenplays or contributed to them, I know what I want to say and what I want audiences to see."

★ ★ ★

David Lean entered "the ranks of the technicians" early in 1928 at the Gainsborough Studios at Shepherds Bush, London, while motion pictures were still mostly without sound. It was an exciting era of British achievements in silent films, soon to be dulled by massive American competition with sound pictures. Like so many directors of his generation, Lean first became enamoured of the movies while as a boy and his "education" in cinema began in the only way possible then (and still the most effective way even in this age of university film courses), by going to see films as often as possible.

He was born in Croydon, a suburb of London, on March 25, 1908, the son of a strict Quaker family which considered going to the pictures to be a sinful pastime. His father was an accountant with a comfortable income. After the First World War was over, when Lean was ten years old, he went to Leighton Park Quaker School in Reading, where he was considered to be "either not very bright or incorrigibly lazy." Away from home, he was free to go to the cinema, which he did several times a week, and photography became his hobby. This knowledge of camerawork acquired so early in life is one of the main reasons for the perfection of cinematography in his pictures.

After leaving school he "drifted" into his father's office as a junior clerk, to begin a career as an accountant. "I added up and checked rows of figures, which at least five other people had added up and checked before. I had the greatest difficulty in arriving at

David Lean in Finland during the shooting of DOCTOR ZHIVAGO.

the same figure as the previous and doubtless more accurate human comptometer." It was from this accounting experience that Lean, although having made some of the most expensive films in movie history, acquired his understanding of economics and familiarity with budgets.

His passion for films grew and at nineteen—with the assistance of his mother and aunt, the latter suggesting that his interest in photography would be better served by films—he threw off all pretentions as to his interest in accountancy, and went along to the Gainsborough Studios (now a part of British cinema history and used by the BBC) and applied for a job. It was a typically drab and cheerless English day with heavy showers, a background to his life which still brings melancholy to him and many Englishmen, no matter where they travel and live. Even today, David Lean, still an ardent photographer, has moody moments when he will photograph sad and dreary landscapes or people, simply because they are "cold and horrible and miserable."

The heady glamour and excitement at being so close to the movies was only slightly diminished by the apparent unimportance of the jobs offered him at Gainsborough Studios: wardrobe assistant; fetching tea for directors; third assistant director (chasing recalcitrant extras around); and even number-board boy—holding the board identifying the beginning of each "take." (Later, with the coming of sound, it became the clapper board.)

It was tiring work, with low pay, which the young Lean carried out with a quiet enthusiasm in a precarious and callous profession. Oddly enough, for all his interest in photography, he did not much favour becoming a cameraman (as they were then called), although he did work for a short time as a camera assistant. He watched and learned, assisted Anthony Asquith, and it became apparent to him that success in knowing and understanding films lay in the cutting and editing rooms, and this in turn, could lead to direction.

In the editing rooms he began by carrying the cans of films. But the anomalies of these early jobs soon ended as he became, first in 1930, assistant editor and then editor, of Gaumont-British sound news and British Movietone News, and then, in 1934, editor of Paramount's British quota quickies—inexpensive feature films made by American companies to meet their British quota obligations. Here he studied every phase and facet of a film in intimate detail together with the marvel of sound reproduction. Every foot of film went through his close inspection, every flaw in the work of the director, actor, cameraman, or sound engineer was visible to him, together with their best work. He became fascinated with the myriad disjointed little strips of film that go to make up a motion picture, and was intrigued by the manner in which they could be joined together, entire sequences built up, rhythm, pace and continuity controlled by cutting, with comedy or drama being heightened and manipulated. Everything Eisenstein had written about became clear in the movieola, and Lean soon developed an unerring eye for the most effective shots, and found he had a gift for editing them into a compelling shape and a lucid continuity. Directors who had not been trained in editing sought him out. His first important dramatic film as an editor was Paul Czinner's *Escape Me Never* in 1936. This was followed by a host of well-known British films of the late Thirties including *Pygmalion,* in 1938. By the time the Second World War had begun in September, 1939, his "movie madness" of the First World War period had brought him the enviable reputation of being the most skilful editor at work in British studios. Everything he had done since 1928 prepared him for the position of director which came to him in 1942, after editing *Major Barbara* and *49th Parallel (The Invaders).*

Noël Coward was preparing to produce and direct a screenplay he had written entitled, *In Which We Serve,* although he had no film experience, and had cast himself in the leading role. He recognised Lean's knowledge and ability and invited him to co-direct the picture with him, a shrewd move since Coward wanted to preserve his own authority and artistic reputation and knew only too well that he would have difficulties working with an established director. He could only benefit however from the experience of a talented film artist who knew all the theory of form and technique, but who had no pre-conceived directorial methods to clash with Coward's ideas. To give Coward his due, he always acknowledged Lean's contribution to the successful outcome of the collaboration.

It was the opportunity for the fusion of all Lean's hard-earned experience, the beginning of his directorial career reached through a dogged determination and singleness of purpose, the cumulative result of the critical, constructive study he had put into his work. He could see actors, sets and scripts, not in the context of the studio floor (although that had been a valuable start), but in the more cerebral way these elements looked and sounded through the camera and registered on strips of film hung up in the editing room.

David Lean saw very clearly where he was going. He was determined that *In Which We Serve* would not be the only film he would work on as a director. The film to follow would certainly

Spiegel, Peter O'Toole, Omar Sharif and Lean
on location for LAWRENCE OF ARABIA.

be edited by him, but he would be editing film he had entirely
directed, perhaps into a new and compelling shape. Always a restless personality, modest and unwilling to talk about himself, he
began to think of new techniques, personalities, stories, to contribute to the new spirit of Britain's reviving film creativity, given an
added impetus by the war. This national emergency made the
British more aware of the need to seek a unity and recognition of
themselves as a nation on the influential cinema screens, previously
dominated by American movies.

"In my career I've been terribly lucky. I came in during the
early years when films were still silent. There were no unions then,
and because of this I had the opportunity of going around the studio
doing all sorts of jobs, from making tea, turning the camera, going
into the editing department, being an assistant director, and at one
time being a wardrobe mistress. This was a background of learn-
ing. I could move around. Today you cannot move around like
that. I suppose you can in the new film schools. I think a background like this is extremely important because if you are intent
on becoming a director you must know the tools of your trade.
I don't know how that's done nowadays in the picture business

because you attach yourself to one department and remain there. It's frightfully difficult to get a good all-round grounding."

★   ★   ★

Because of the once clearly defined lines between the social classes in Britain, few British films until the coming of the "angry young men" authors and actors, could escape the "drawing room" atmosphere and elegance of British society as it was reflected mainly in the theatre and carried over into the cinema. It was a world of "lower orders" and "upper classes," the truth and honesty of which was frequently lost in stereotypes, but fundamentally, could not be denied. This has been disturbing to many critics over the years, who have written agonisingly and not always convincingly about British social attitudes and character in the cinema resulting from class consciousness. No other nation has had so much trouble in its films with class distinction as the British. However, as society changes, British films have taken on the glossy characteristics of the international scene, leaving behind the squire and the country pub, becoming a cinema in which James Bond can be well-educated and a connoisseur yet not speak with an Oxford accent. In some ways, native qualities have been lost, not always replaced with satisfying substitutes. But the youth of Britain today is not that of Children's Film Foundation pictures.

David Lean, whose work has reflected the English social scene more acutely perhaps than many other directors, has never been involved in a British film that did not concern the classes, partly as a result of working with or from authors whose snob values or social significances are their recognised themes: Noël Coward; Charles Dickens; H. G. Wells; Terence Rattigan; Harold Brighouse; and T. E. Lawrence. Not until his first American film, *Summertime*, did Lean make an unconsciously classless film. Class returned with the British army of Lawrence and Colonel Nicholson, and he had Russian upper and lower orders to contend with in *Doctor Zhivago*, containing a revolution entirely motivated by class upheaval, and it was class in the army again which intruded into the Irish working-class village life of *Ryan's Daughter*.

This has been one of two prevailing characteristics in Lean's work. The second is his personal predilection for portraying the passionate emotions of romantic people in love, and the extreme acts they are driven to and the torments they suffer in their sexual desires and encounters. Since *Brief Encounter*, none of the principals of Lean's films, in which love between men and women is the main theme, have ever been happily in love except for Mossop and

Maggie in *Hobson's Choice*. Most of them are married, but marriage does not seem to have brought them happiness or satisfaction. It is easy to call Lean "a romantic director" of "love stories" except that this is not true. To romanticise is to delight in what is fanciful, and to be a romantic in art is to place more value on imagination and fancy than on things as they are. Lean may be imaginative in his use of film, and his characters may indulge in romanticising in imagination a life quite different from the one they are living, but his stories, people and events are all very real figures in very real places, times, and situations.

Looking at Lean this way we find a strong, brooding, poetic creator with an over-riding love of adventure, of women as dangerous creatures, and of the cinema as the most expressive art form, the latter being the means to quicken the stories of other lives once lived, and of lives being acted out around him. His spirit as an artist is not a result of nationality; but his awareness of class consciousness does come from being English, and in telling stories of mostly British people rooted in their community and class standards.

Peter O'Toole and David Lean enjoy a joke during filming.

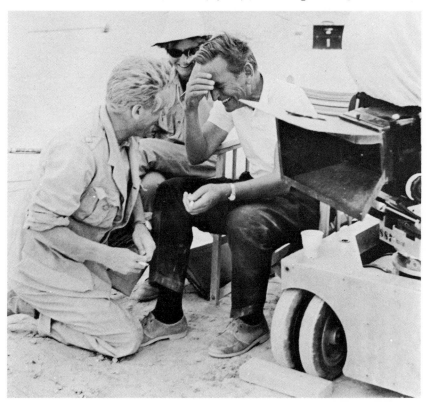

"I'm really still an editor at heart. I can't keep my hands off the scissors. It's a wonderful feeling, handling film, because for the first time, when the film is cut, when I start cutting the close-ups into the long shots and the close-ups against close-ups, and the many variations of this, you start to see if all the work you did as a director is, in fact, working. There's another blessing about it which is that after six months or a year sometimes more surrounded by this great circus of mine, it's wonderful to sit quietly in a room with the film. Then at times like this, I think back to other films and other places, to matters right outside the films themselves. I'll never forget being in the desert and living in a caravan for a year, miles away from anywhere, or a year in the forests of Ceylon, or the way I've got to know Venice and Spain, and all the various trips I've taken looking for locations. They're exciting; like gigantic holidays when one was a boy."

DAVID LEAN

1. In Which We Serve (1942)

Directors: Noël Coward and David Lean. *Screenplay:* Noël Coward. *Photography:* Ronald Neame. *Camera Operator:* Guy Green. *Art Director:* David Rawnsley. *Art Supervisor* (to Noël Coward): G. E. Calthrop. *Editor:* Thelma Myers. *Sound:* C. C. Stevens. *Re-recording:* Desmond Dew. *Unit Manager:* Michael Anderson. *Music:* Noël Coward. *Producer:* Noël Coward. *Associate Producer:* Anthony Havelock-Allan. *Production:* Two Cities Films. *Release:* British Lion. October 1, 1942. 10,270 ft. 113 minutes.

CAST

Captain "D"	Noël Coward
O/S "Shorty" Blake	John Mills
CPO Walter Hardy	Bernard Miles
Alix, Mrs. Kinross	Celia Johnson
Mrs. Hardy	Joyce Carey
Freda Lewis	Kay Walsh
Number One	Derek Elphinstone
"Flags"	Michael Wilding
"Guns"	Robert Sansom
"Torps"	Philip Friend
Doctor	James Donald

Engineer Commander	Ballard Berkeley
"Snotty"	Chimmo Branson
Sub-Lieut. RNVR	Kenneth Carten
Mr. Blake	George Carney
Mrs. Blake	Kathleen Harrison
Uncle Fred	Wally Patch
Young Stoker	Richard Attenborough
Maureen Fenwick	Penelope Dudley Ward
Pilot	Hubert Gregg
Edgecombe	Frederick Piper
Brodie	Caven Watson
Coxswain	Johnnie Schofield
A/B Joey Mackridge	Geoffrey Hibbert
A/B Hollett	John Boxer
Parkinson	Leslie Dwyer
Col. Lumsden	Walter Fitzgerald
Capt. Jasper Fry	Gerald Case
Mrs. Lemmon	Dora Gregory
Reynolds	Lionel Grosse
Mrs. Scatterthwaite	Norma Pierce
Lavinia	Ann Stephens
Bobby	Daniel Massey
May Blake	Jill Stephens
Mrs. Farrell	Eileen Peele
Mrs. Macadoo	Barbara Waring
Barmaid	Kay Young
Freda's Baby	Juliet Mills

Story

A drama of the British Navy, describing the fortunes of a destroyer and three members of its crew from the time of the launching until it meets a gallant end at sea. The principal characters are the captain (Noël Coward), a chief petty officer (Bernard Miles), and an ordinary seaman (John Mills), whose adventures, both domestic and maritime, are given in flashback sequences after their ship has gone down fighting off the coast of Crete.

David Lean

"When I was an editor and cutter, I became a kind of film doctor in which producers would give me films they thought were very

"Shorty" Blake (John Mills) says goodbye to his wife (Kay Walsh).

hard to edit or had been cut by someone else, not too successfully perhaps, and I would put them together. Apparently I did it well. At this time I started getting various offers to direct small pictures called 'quota-quickies' made by the Americans for a pound a foot. One of the wisest things I ever did was to say 'No.' They were made in three weeks, the director didn't have a chance, and if the film was a disaster no one said, 'Well, remember he did it in only three weeks, he had terrible actors and an incompetent director.' Few people today remember that time. So I turned all these offers down until Noël Coward came along. He was about to make a film about the navy, *In Which We Serve*, and needed a co-director. He asked all sorts of people and several of them mentioned my name. He offered me the job, naturally I jumped at it, and I'm glad to say it was successful."

Comment

It is important to remember, looking at this remarkable film thirty years after it was made, that it is a motion picture about war made in wartime, during a period of history when no one spoke about "anti"-war films. It reflected quite accurately the sentiments of the three classes which made up British society, the

*Captain "D" (Noël Coward) leaves his wife
(Celia Johnson) and children for battle.*

working, middle and upper class, in the simplified way in which
all people then looked at war. Although it included the first defeat in Europe, with the evacuation of mostly British forces at
Dunkirk, and "Hitler's Entry Into Paris," it was still a time when
almost everybody, in spite of the desert war, the air raids and the
Battle of Britain still thought that the ultimate horrors of war were
the Flanders fields trench battles of the First World War, and
which, despite Hitler's strategy, would probably be the pattern
the Second World War would follow.

The subsequent and savage allied campaigns and encounters with
the enemy throughout all of Europe, the tank battles, the assault
on Russia and the starvation of Leningrad, the mass destruction of
cities by aerial bombardment, the horrors of the Japanese theatre

John Mills proposes a toast at the Blake family's Christmas party.

of war, culminating in the ghastly mind-defeating agonies of the concentration camps, were all aspects of war totally unthought of in 1942, where the war at sea, revolving around the sinking of vital supply ships by U-boats (as in the First War) again reinforced sub-conscious ideas that this Second War was bound to be similar to the first. As a result, it was quite natural that Hitler could be referred to in the film in the same semi-friendly way as "Kaiser Bill" was in the other war. It does seem unbelievable today to look at Noël Coward as the captain of a ship's destroyer and hear him conclude his exhortation to the crew to get the ship ready for sailing in three weeks with the declaration that "we'll then send a telegram to Hitler saying he can start his war at any time;" and later, when the wife of Bernard Miles is telling the crotchety old mother on the stairs that war is imminent and she replies "who does Hitler think he is?" In other words, the appalling evils still to be unleashed by the barbaric acts of war were unthinkable, and it made possible a concept of war which, as portrayed in *In Which We Serve,* was both admirable and realistic at that time.

The film begins in Grierson documentary form with a montage of scenes showing the building of the destroyer, with close-ups of workers' faces, of rivets being driven into steel plates, sections of the ship being swung into place, the keel taking shape, culminating in the champagne bottle breaking on the bow and the ship sliding into the water. The entire sequence, accompanied by cleverly integrated music and sound effects, is powerful and convincing, and is rapidly followed by a series of fast-moving, quickly edited, shots of the destroyer undergoing trials, with the sea racing past the bows and the side of the ship in great waves, beautifully photographed by Ronald Neame. While there is little in this prelude which had not been seen before in British documentary films, it is an exciting introduction to the style and sensitivity of a new director, not Noël Coward, but David Lean, who, being fairly unknown to critics and public at the time this film was shown, was scarcely mentioned in any reviews. The feeling for movement and lyricism within the frame of each shot and the skilful editing and cross-cutting was to become a characteristic in many of Lean's films to follow. The sea with its spray and the sky with its clouds is a beautiful example of black-and-white photography and feeling for the elements. After this realism it requires a considerable adjustment to come back to earth with Noël Coward as the imperturbable captain of HMS Torrens shouting "fire" amid shot and shell as he engages the enemy

Chief Petty Officer Hardy (Bernard Miles)
and "Shorty" Blake (John Mills) meet on board.

Captain (Noël Coward) and crew cling to the life-raft after the sinking of the destroyer.

in a fierce bombardment off the island of Crete. The familiar "bridge" scenes with the captain and his officers, binoculars around their necks, staring out to battle, are very obviously studio sets, with the mock-up of the ship's bridge mounted on rockers and being moved backwards and forwards in exactly the same measured distance no matter how the waves varied. However, the fact is that at the time this film was made, in the days of the old standard screen and when colour was a rarity, few moviegoers knew much about film fakery or even noticed the artificiality of these scenes. Seen years later, after the advent of the wide-screen and location filming, they become suspect. Yet, in spite of these studio "tank" battles, the explosions with their attendant carnage, killing and wounding, are most life-like, due to Lean's close-up photography, editing and imaginative use of sound.

A series of appropriately "watery" flashbacks follow as the destroyer sinks and the three main characters, the captain (Noël Coward), the officer (Bernard Miles), and the ordinary seaman (John Mills) struggle to reach the life-raft, save their companions, and dodge the bullets of low-flying enemy aircraft. As each moment appears to be their last, they recall scenes from their home life. Coward is very stilted with Celia Johnson (her high-pitched English voice sounding rather old-fashioned today) and their two

A typically "Coward" situation in IN WHICH WE SERVE. The crew of H.M.S. Torrens after their rescue.

children living in the country house; Bernard Miles is comfortable, understanding, entirely believable in his middle-class home with wife, Joyce Carey, making tea and patiently dealing with the complaining old mother upstairs; and John Mills is a delightfully common cockney, honest and out-going, "living it up" with his screeching old mum, Kathleen Harrison, and his garrulous relatives, arguing the merits of the fighting forces over the proverbial cup of tea. A wedding, an air raid, Dunkirk, and other incidents, are cleverly included in the complicated narrative which links the lives of the survivors and their shared experiences with the war, the ship, the sea, and their survival. Throughout, British documentary realism is apparent in scenes showing ammunition being brought up from the magazine, deck by deck, and loaded into the guns. Here we meet another young player—who is to become a great actor and director in British films—Richard Attenborough, as the panic-stricken young rating. Later, he is magnanimously forgiven by Captain Coward. Although Noël Coward deserves much credit for having made this film, the truly humanitarian moments in the picture, although written by him, are not to be found in his scenes, but in those acted by Miles and Mills. Both were to become superb actors, but even in this early work they were extremely natural and effective throughout, particularly in the scene where Mills tells Bernard Miles that his beloved wife has been killed in an air raid. The air raid itself is also memorable as Kay Walsh, Joyce Howard and Dora Gregory sit together in the parlour of their home in Plymouth, trying to control their fears, speaking Coward's outwardly ordinary but effective dialogue, and listening to the noise of airplane engines coming nearer, the whole ending in a devastating explosion.

Another memorable scene, and one that has an echo in Lean's *Bridge on the River Kwai*, shows the wounded soldiers from Dunkirk lining up on the deck after leaving the destroyer, and marching away, with intercut close-ups of the sailors' faces watching them. There is a clever use of camera, and an early indication of Lean's method in the scene showing Kathleen Harrison almost running with a telegram to Kay Walsh informing her that her husband, John Mills, is safe. She moves through the kitchen and into the parlour, the camera at first seeing her through a glass partition and then tracking back into the parlour itself.

The final farewell scene is somewhat static as the Captain comes to say goodbye to his men, who are being assigned to other ships. The theme, however, "that we must take up the battle with a

*Return of wounded Dunkirk soldiers shows
Lean's use of documentary style realism.*

stronger heart," was tremendously stirring to audiences in this time
of war, and the emotional impact of the entire film, in which civilians and fighting men were shown to be sharing a common experience necessary for their survival, was one of love of fellow country-
men and a devotion to a necessary cause.

In Which We Serve is a film of authority, skill and technical
command, and most important, in retrospect, is its place in British
cinema, where, under wartime stress, audiences became aware of
themselves on the screen as a nation of people with much to contribute to the drama of life, hitherto thought to be the exclusive
preserve of American and European film-makers. David Lean's
contribution to this new era in artistic expression in the cinema was
considerable. Having begun with it, he rapidly became one of its
leading directors.

Three of the men who worked with Lean on this film went on to
become directors: Ronald Neame, the cameraman, Guy Green, the
camera operator, and Michael Anderson, the unit manager.

2. This Happy Breed (1944)

Director: David Lean. *Screenplay:* Noël Coward, from his own play. *Photography:* Ronald Neame (Technicolor). *Art Director:* C. P. Norman. *Editor:* Jack Harris. *Sound:* C. C. Stevens. *Musical Director:* Muir Mathieson. *Production Manager:* K. Horne and J. Martin. *Camera Operator:* Guy Green. *Art Supervisor (to Noël Coward):* G. E. Calthrop. *Producer:* Noël Coward. *Production:* Two Cities. *Release:* Eagle-Lion, Gaumont, Haymarket, London, June 1, 1944. 9,939 ft. 111 mins.

CAST

Frank Gibbons	Robert Newton
Ethel Gibbons	Celia Johnson
Billy Mitchell	John Mills
Queenie Gibbons	Kay Walsh
Mrs. Flint	Amy Vennes
Aunt Sylvia	Alison Leggatt
Vi	Eileen Erskine
Reg	John Blythe
Bob Mitchell	Stanley Holloway
Sam Leadbitter	Guy Verney
Phyllis	Betty Fleetwood
Edie	Merle Tottenham

Story

It is the close of the First World War. Frank has just been demobbed. He has served for four years and is eager to return to his wife and children. He rescues his wife Ethel and his children from the house they have been sharing with his mother-in-law, and they all move into 17, Sycamore Road, Clapham. Aunt Syl and Grandma Flint come too, of course, to the new house.

The house is soon divided up into its vital little areas—"Reg's room" at the top of the stairs, the "parlour," the Hall, and "the cupboard under the stairs." Ethel tidies up the home while Frank transforms his small backyard into "the Gibbonses' Garden." Percy, the cat, becomes the virtual owner of the back fence.

Aunt Syl takes up various "isms" in a pathetic effort to allay her frustrated longing for marriage and motherhood, and to help stave off the barbs of the malicious Mrs. Flint. The children grow up. Queenie goes to work in a smart West End beauty parlour. Reg gets into trouble over the General Strike and comes home to his mother with a cut eye. But soon he is getting married—to little Phyllis. The wedding is a grand affair, but not long afterwards, Reg is killed in a car crash.

Then Queenie runs off with a married man, instead of following family expectations and settling down with Billy, the sailor boy who lives next door. But later Billy and Queenie meet again, for the Gibbons's daughter has been badly let down by her lover, and the two get married after all. Their baby, little Frankie, is born, and when Queenie goes to Singapore to join her sailor husband, he is left in the care of his grandparents. With everyone leaving the house in Sycamore Road, the old folks decide to move to a self-contained flat. As they prepare to leave, with little Frankie in the pram, Frank puts his arm around his wife and says that it doesn't matter where they go, as long as they remain together.

David Lean

"When I was a tea boy, I never intentionally thought of becoming a director, because I thought it was over some vast, distant horizon. Now I am a director, I think only of becoming a better director with each film. Noël Coward was very generous. He didn't really enjoy film direction. He liked writing and acting best, and by the time *In Which We Serve* was finished he said, 'Well dear boy, you can take anything I write and make a film of it.' The outcome of this was a partnership with Anthony Havelock-Allan and

*Robert Newton, Celia Johnson and Alison Leggatt
arrive at their new home in THIS HAPPY BREED.*

Ronald Neame in a company we called Cineguild, and three films
from Noël's plays. The first, *This Happy Breed,* was my first experience alone with actors. The first thing I remembered from the
advice he had given me was to understand the characters in the
script. He said: 'You've got to know what every character eats for
breakfast even though you should never show them eating breakfast.' You've got to know what sort of people they are. Would they
do this or that? It's a question of taste with characters, it's like
knowing a living human being. Once you understand this, you
know what you want from the actors, and as most of them are
very good, working with them is not difficult."

Comment

This is Noël Coward's lower-class *Cavalcade,* the story of the
Gibbons family between two world wars, played by Robert Newton and Celia Johnson. Newton, a magnificent master of character
parts, often larger-than-life but commanding in their truth, was
never again quite as restrained as he was here playing what Coward
considered to be the "family man." Miss Johnson, down a class from

*Frank Gibbons (Robert Newton) and Ethel Gibbons
(Celia Johnson) in a scene from THIS HAPPY BREED.*

*The Gibbons busy themselves while Mrs. Flint
(Amy Vennes) looks on despondently.*

In Which We Serve, plays the understanding wife who is nevertheless a good deal more intelligent than her husband, but never in such a way as to let him know it. Kay Walsh is back as one of the Gibbons's children, and John Mills returns to play the son of the next-door neighbour, a part taken by Stanley Holloway. Coward would have us believe that what we see in *This Happy Breed* is the essential humour of the Londoner, the courage, the wit, the simple philosophy of little people living in little houses. A lot of it is true, due largely to the actors, who engagingly provide happy touches of character and a delicate play of sensibility to illuminate the events which touch their lives. But Coward in his writing is not so much pushed by the force of war, so that he becomes detached and patronising. His view of history is exasperating; he plays to the new enjoyment of British audiences, the pleasure of recognition of themselves. He wants to compliment them, but he almost caricatures them. David Lean tones it down, establishing a warm and believable atmosphere, and as a statement of British middle-class life, the film still ranks high, much imitated and castigated, yet undeniably holding a place in the affections of the older generation. Its reality grows out of the recognisability of people liked for their sincere virtues of kindness and friendliness.

This Happy Breed (a title taken from John of Gaunt's speech in Shakespeare's *Richard II*) was the first film in the new partnership of David Lean, Anthony Havelock-Allan and Ronald Neame. Lean had met Havelock-Allan when both worked at Paramount before the war, and Neame came up through the studios to be a cameraman in much the same way Lean had. It was Havelock-Allan, with Filippo Del Giudice of Two Cities Films, who had suggested to Noël Coward (until then a man of the theatre) that he write a film story. The result was *In Which We Serve*. Havelock-Allan suggested Lean as Coward's associate director, and Neame as cameraman. Thus the three came together. They formed Cineguild, and Coward, being immensely pleased with the success of *In Which We Serve*, gave them permission to film *This Happy Breed*, *Blithe Spirit* and *Brief Encounter*. Cineguild, working for Two Cities Films, which in turn were distributed by General Film Distributors and Eagle Lion, played a vital part in a tremendously productive, exciting era of independent film-making under the encouraging banner of the new J. Arthur Rank Organisation. There were the Archers (Michael Powell and Emeric Pressburger); Individual Pictures (Frank Launder and Sidney Gilliat); Charter Films (The Boulting Brothers); Ealing Studios; and Gainsborough Studios, and the films

*Alison Leggatt and Celia Johnson in a
scene from THIS HAPPY BREED.*

of the time ranged from *Fanny by Gaslight* to *One of Our Aircraft
Is Missing, I Know Where I'm Going, The Rake's Progress, Dead
of Night, It Never Rains on Sunday, Half Way House, Henry V,
Pink String and Sealing Wax, Waterloo Road, The Way to the Stars,*
and many others, all fondly remembered as part of a great era now
gone, a time when British studios had a recognised individuality,
when British film-makers found themselves and their audience, and
created a native cinema. At the time *This Happy Breed* was made
there were only four Technicolor cameras in England. Lean's second film, and first as the complete director, was also his first in
colour. This was the time when British film-makers were said to
use colour with a delicacy and realism never found in American
movies, which tended to emphasise bright and garish hues. Colour
in British wartime films was used as an integral part of the interpretation of the narrative, and the reticence of its expression in *This
Happy Breed* so enhanced the realistic effect that it was hardly
noticed by audiences.

The essence of Lean's cinematic style and way of thinking is
apparent throughout the film. It never looks like a filmed play, nor
does it go to extremes to deny its theatrical origin. As illustration,
the following sequence shows Lean's imagination at work: The

Stanley Holloway as the next-door neighbour,
and Robert Newton savouring the fish paste.

Queenie Gibbons (Kay Walsh) with her mother (Celia Johnson).

daughter comes into the living room with the news that her brother and his wife have been killed in a motor car accident. She tells her grandmother, who is in the room, and who then leaves. The room is empty, the parents being outside in the garden. The girl goes out into the garden through the French windows. The camera now moves to reveal more of the garden, until it can go no further. No cut is made to the garden. We wait in the empty room, well able to imagine what is being said outside. After an unendurable moment, the grief-stricken mother and father come slowly in and sit down. A literal depiction of such a terrible, but also simple moment could not possibly be more moving or believable than this little gem of content by implication.

Billy Mitchell (John Mills) comforts a weeping Ethel Gibbons (Celia Johnson).

3. Blithe Spirit (1945)

Director: David Lean. *Screenplay:* Noël Coward, from his play. *Photography:* Ronald Neame (Technicolor). *Art Director:* C. P. Norman. *Editor:* Jack Harris. *Sound:* John Cooke. *Re-recording:* Desmond Dew. *Camera Operator:* W. McLeod. *Music:* Richard Addinsell. *Associate Producer:* Anthony Havelock-Allan. *Assistant Director:* George Pollock. *Unit Manager:* Norman Spencer. *Production:* Cineguild-Two Cities. *Release:* General Film Distributors, Odeon, Leicester Square, London, April 5, 1945. 8,609 ft. 96 minutes.

CAST

Condomine	Rex Harrison
Elvira	Constance Cummings
Ruth	Kay Hammond
Madame Arcati	Margaret Rutherford
Dr. Bradman	Hugh Wakefield
Mrs. Bradman	Joyce Carey
Edith, the Maid	Jacqueline Clarke

Condomine (Rex Harrison) and his second wife Ruth (Kay Hammond) in a scene from BLITHE SPIRIT.

Margaret Rutherford as the medium conducts a seance. Left to right: Rutherford, Hammond, Harrison, Carey and Wakefield.

Story

Sophisticated comedy of the macabre, freely adapted from Noël Coward's stage success, in which the eternal triangle theme is interpreted from a frivolous spirit-world existence. An English novelist (Rex Harrison) invites a medium (Margaret Rutherford) to his home for a seance and as a result, his first wife (Constance Cummings) materialises, much to the annoyance of his second wife (Kay Hammond), who enlists the aid of the medium, Madame Arcati, to send Elvira back to the supernatural world. Elvira arranges a car accident to kill Condomine so that he could be with her. But Ruth is in the car and she is killed instead, and also returns as a ghost. Condomine, exasperated by the presence of two ghostly wives, decides to leave them and departs in the car. This time, both wives have manipulated the car, again there is an accident, he is killed, and has to cope with both of his wives on "the other side."

David Lean

"The time was right for a comedy. People had endured the darkness of war; we had done two films which, while not without humour, were about the trials and tribulations of wartime and daily life. Noël, who taught me a great deal of what I know, had said earlier, 'always come out of another hole,' by which he meant if you do a story like *Cavalcade* follow it with something completely different. I enjoyed making this film; being part fantasy it was a technical as well as an artistic challenge, and considering the shortages and problems which plagued the studios at that time I think the special effects worked very well."

Comment

The only outright comedy film David Lean has made in his long career is his third Coward picture, *Blithe Spirit*, a quite daring (for its time) divertissement on the hallowed subject of death and spiritualism. The play, having run for five years on the London stage, was a comedy of such longstanding vitality and popularity that much depended on Lean's treatment of it. But with thoughtfulness and intelligence, he came through with an immensely tasteful and brilliantly funny picture, as much at ease with Coward's prewar cynical manner and frivolous, heartless people as he had been with the "commonplace" lives of the "ordinary" people. In *Blithe Spirit*,

*Condomine's ghostly first wife (Constance Cummings),
threatens him with a chair.*

Rex Harrison added to his rapidly growing reputation as a romantic
lover, a ladies' man, in the role of a writer, living comfortably in
the country with his second wife, who is suddenly visited by the
ghostly figure of his mischievous first wife, visible only to him.

Lean again uses colour effectively: the ghostly presence of Kay
Hammond is indicated in green. Margaret Rutherford became
known to film audiences all over the world as a result of playing
Madame Arcati, the eccentric medium, who rode her bicycle to and
from the village. With this picture, Lean asserted himself as a
sophisticated artist bringing high comedy to British cinema. As
with *This Happy Breed,* there was little indication of the play's
stage origin. Lean's perceptive film sense was already strikingly
obvious.

4. Brief Encounter (1945)

Director: David Lean. *Screenplay:* Noël Coward, based on his play "Still Life" from "Tonight at 8.30." *Photography:* Robert Krasker. *Art Direction:* L. P. Williams. *Editor:* Jack Harris. *Sound:* Stanley Lambourne and Desmond Dew. *Re-recording:* Desmond Dew. *In charge of production:* Anthony Havelock-Allan and Ronald Neame. *Assistant Director:* George Pollock. *Production:* Cineguild. *Music:* Rachmaninov's Piano Concerto No. 2 played by Eileen Joyce, with the National Symphony Orchestra conducted by Muir Mathieson. *Release:* Eagle-Lion. November 26, 1945. New Gallery Cinema, London. 7,713 ft. 86 minutes. *Prix International de Critique, Cannes 1946.*

CAST

Laura Jesson	Celia Johnson
Dr. Alec Harvey	Trevor Howard
Fred Jesson	Cyril Raymond
Albert Godby	Stanley Holloway
Myrtle Bagot	Joyce Carey
Beryl Waters	Margaret Barton
Stephen Lynn	Valentine Dyall

Dolly Messiter	Beverly Gregg
Mrs. Rolandson	Nuna Davey
Clergyman	George V. Sheldon
Boatman	Jack May
Bill	Edward Hodge
Policeman	Wilfred Babbage
Margaret	Henrietta Vincent
Stanley	Dennis Harkin
Mary Norton	Marjorie Mars
Organist	Irene Handl
Johnnie	Sydney Bromley
Waitress	Avis Scutt
Bobbie	Richard Thomas
Doctor	Wally Bosco

Story

A domestic drama, the self-told story of Laura Jesson, a country housewife, securely and sometimes suffocatingly tied down to her husband and children, who goes into town to do her weekly shopping, and meets and falls in love with a young doctor. The meetings and farewells take place in a dingy railway station, the junction for many suburban trains. After several meetings, they go to the flat belonging to a friend of the doctor's, but are interrupted by the friend's unexpected return. They realise that a future together is impossible and agree to part.

David Lean

"I had discovered that every film is in a way a prototype. You begin with nothing on your hands, you start absolutely from scratch and it's very frightening. I find that the first two weeks I do on any movie are bad. I know I'm over-meticulous and I worry too much. After a few weeks the film starts to take over. I know where to put the camera, how to talk to the actors. In a way it's luck, but you won't have any luck if you haven't got a good script. Luckily, Noël proved to be very good at adapting his plays to the screen. We all worked with him, of course. The dialogue was always his. One of my great fears was being on the set, running a rehearsal, and something unexpected crops up. An idea which seemed brilliant doesn't work, and it's difficult to think of another

Laura Jesson (Celia Johnson) meets Dr. Harvey
(Trevor Howard) in BRIEF ENCOUNTER.

way of doing it. A kind of mental paralysis sets in. I suppose directors are like actors. They have to pretend a bit more, although I suppose we all pretend that we are more confident than we are."

Comment

In an age of easy conscience and mild morality, it is hard for some people to believe that a man and a woman could be torn to pieces by an illicit love. Yet *Brief Encounter* is as believable today as it was on its first showing. More than this, there are still men and women who would behave in just the same way, even if the social climate has changed sufficiently that they might conceivably have an affair and not suffer the pangs of guilt and remorse. The point is that the prevailing social order has very little to do with it. Human maturity lies at the crux of the problem. Laura Jesson and Dr. Alec Harvey might well fall romantically in love with each other, but it would be impossible for them to hurt their families, impossible for them to be happy together, because of their inbred feelings of morality and guilt, their principles and devotion. For this reason, *Brief Encounter* remains as true today as when it was first written. Of all the four films Lean has made from Coward's

Lean's dramatic lighting heightens the lovers' dismal situation.

The train is a familiar Lean symbol of departure and loss.
Celia Johnson and Trevor Howard in BRIEF ENCOUNTER.

work, this is the most completely honest and effective. When it was released, David Lean was recognised as an outstanding film-maker. It was praised with such remarks as "more like a French film" (the highest commendation in those days) and "an emotionally-grown up British picture." This astonishingly simple, sincere work, so commonplace, uncomfortably true, and deeply affecting, is actually an extraordinarily clever piece of film-making, based on a tight but complex pattern of flashbacks, evocative thoughts, a softly spoken narration, a marvellously emotional use of music (Rachmaninov's Concerto No. 2), the sound of trains rushing through the station, of arriving and departing—all producing a never-failing perceptive, sympathetic and observant study of character. The only weaknesses are the synthetic cockneys in the synthetic station buffet played by Stanley Holloway and Joyce Carey, the comedy of the lower orders once more rendered in caricature. (They are always on duty it seems.)

The theme is one of the most difficult for both writer and director to express with sincerity and credibility. One false step, and the entire logicality of the venture collapses into absurdity, simply because the behaviour of these two nice respectable, married, people is absurd; but not to them, only to outside observers. Although we

Stanley Holloway and Joyce Carey . . . "always on duty."

come to recognise the absurdity of their behaviour and what they say, we still believe in them. This David Lean makes us do with a great sensitivity as Laura and Alec are driven from happy coffee encounters in the waiting room to furtive visits to the cinema, always afraid of the chance meeting with friends, driven to small deceits that tarnish the joy of the first encounter, finally arriving at the point where a room is necessary—the culminating aim of the entire exercise, whether consciously or not. Here, it must be remembered, censorship was extremely rigid at this time. It is a small marvel the film was ever made, that they actually kissed, that they got as far as the flat of a friend. It was the arrival of the friend unexpectedly that made fulfillment impossible. Cynics would say it was dramatically devised to avoid censorship. Perhaps this is so, but it is a perfectly plausible situation which causes a deepening feeling of shame and humiliation on the part of such a couple for allowing themselves to become the victims of circumstances. Here for the first time, was the expression of a theme to be found in five of Lean's films yet to come; the temptations of passion, "the animal which is only a little way under our skins which can be very exciting but very dangerous."

Insight, detachment, and style mark this picture throughout, yet it is never cold or unfeeling. The splendid shots of the trains in the station, the express trains going far away perhaps, to other places warmer and more alive; the dismal local train gliding in and out, its carriage windows glowing with the lights of imaginary romanticism in which Laura sees herself dancing with Alec at a sumptuous ball, the shrieks of the whistle, the silences following departures, these are all achingly real, and filmed in a real station. The studio created waiting room is real only when we are watching Celia Johnson and Trevor Howard, simply because they are so real we only notice the unreality of the background when attention is turned to Joyce Carey and Stanley Holloway, with their false humour—which is not to deny the professionalism of their performances.

Much of the sensitivity and credibility of the love scenes is due to the acting of Celia Johnson, who, in this third film with Lean, without make-up and cinematic glamour, and without the conventional good looks, portrays the wife and mother with great strength and character. Not only is she effective as the woman herself, but her off-screen narration is spoken with such tenderness that it is difficult to believe she is acting. When she says, "I'm a happily married woman, it was enough, until a few weeks ago . . . I'm an ordinary woman," she is attempting to convince herself that this

Cyril Raymond as the kindly husband more interested in the crossword than his wife.

passion she is experiencing for the first time in her married life, a feeling she is afraid of for fear it will lead her into disaster rather than bring her happiness, is entirely wrong, and she struggles to maintain her outward calm and dignity which all along conceal the destruction going on within her for the sake of decency and propriety. There will be no romantic trips to Venice, no days and nights of eternal love, all life comes back to the same monotony. Yet she will suffer because the promise was there and it might have been realised. Thus, she can say with real feeling, "This misery can't last." She wants "to remember every minute to the end of my days." And she is left with the knowledge that the doctor will be gone, but she will return to the same railway station, the same cinema, teashop and waiting room. "I shall see all this again but without Alec." For Celia Johnson, this was undoubtedly her greatest achievement. Trevor Howard, making his third film, is boyishly good and believable. Not knowing the conditions of his home life as well as Laura Jesson's, there is the thought that he was partly looking for adventure and that, as with most men, if the consummation had taken place, his interest in her would begin to wane.

As for Lean's direction, this is filled with constantly imaginative touches; the first kiss at the station entrance at night, doomed by the long shadows that darken the wall behind them; the swirling newspapers; the coming of rain which marks the beginning of the sad end; the clouds of steam from the trains; the living room fading in behind the outline of Laura in her chair in the corner of the room; these are only a few of many masterly touches. Beautiful to watch, the strength of this film lies in the controlled realism of its details. In the end, we realise that we have seen not a love story but a story of love humiliated by the attitudes of Laura and Alec who, as individuals, cannot believe that love between them is possible on a happy basis, that they could be lovers and enjoy it and still fulfill their obligations to their family. As Laura says about the affair, "the first awful feelings of danger swept over me." She is tormented by guilt feelings, and there is nowhere they can go to be lovers under decent conditions. They both surrender to humiliation and give up, even to the extent that she for a moment contemplates suicide, by throwing herself under one of the trains that have brought them together in the first place. So, saying to herself that such a love affair "doesn't bring happiness," Laura Jesson returns to the quiet country home, the children and her books, to read of other romances of the kind she had just abandoned. And yet, Fred, her husband, with his crossword puzzles was the kind of man whom Alan Sillitoe later described in *Saturday Night and Sunday Morning* as "a slow husband." All Fred wanted was his dinner! He wasn't even interested when Laura told him she had met the doctor.

5. Great Expectations (1946)

Director: David Lean. *Screenplay:* David Lean and Ronald Neame, adapted from the book by Charles Dickens. *Photography:* Guy Green. *Editor:* Jack Harris. Production designer: John Bryan. *Art Director:* Wilfred Shingleton. *Costumes:* Sophia Harris (Motley) and Margaret Furse. *Music:* Walter Goehr, conducting the National Symphony Orchestra. *Sound:* Stanley Lambourne. *Re-recording:* Desmond Dew. *Assistant Director:* George Pollock. *Executive Producer:* Anthony Havelock-Allan. *Producer:* Ronald Neame. *Production:* Cineguild, for the J. Arthur Rank Organisation. *Release:* General Film Distributors, Gaumont and Marble Arch Pavilion, London. December 25, 1946. (US: Universal International. Radio City Music Hall, April 24, 1947.) 10,624 ft. 118 minutes.

CAST

Pip (grown up)	John Mills
Estella (grown up)	Valerie Hobson
Joe Gargery	Bernard Miles
Jaggers	Francis L. Sullivan
Magwitch	Finlay Currie

Miss Havisham	Martita Hunt
Pip (as a boy)	Anthony Wager
Estella (as a girl)	Jean Simmons
Herbert Pocket	Alec Guinness
Pale Young Gentleman	John Forrest
Wemmick	Ivor Barnard
Mrs. Joe Gargery	Freda Jackson
Bentley Drummle	Torin Thatcher
Biddy	Eileen Erskine
Uncle Pumblechook	Hay Petrie
Compeyson	George Hayes
The Sergeant	Richard George
Sarah Pocket	Everly Gregg
Mr. Wopsle	John Burch
Mrs. Wopsle	Grace Denbigh-Russell
The Aged Parent	O. B. Clarence

Note: Francis L. Sullivan played Jaggers in the 1934 version filmed by Universal in Hollywood.

Story

The film adaptation covers first the relations of the boy Pip to Magwitch, the escaped convict whom he helps before his recapture and exile to New South Wales, and to the demented Miss Havisham and her ward Estella. Then the grown Pip receives his fortune from an unknown benefactor, develops in adult life his love for Estella, and finds out his benefactor is Magwitch when the latter illegally returns to visit him in London. Magwitch dies in prison after attempting a futile escape by packet steamer, assisted by Pip and Herbert Pocket, and the lawyer Jaggers reveals that Estella is the convict's daughter. Pip finally rescues her from incipient madness similar to that of Miss Havisham, who has been burnt to death in her decaying mansion.

David Lean

"The film director has the same problem that any storyteller has, and that is to capture the attention of his audience. There's a wonderful opening to the novel, *Death of My Aunt*. It starts something like this: "It was three o'clock in the afternoon when I decided to murder my aunt." By that very sentence, the reader is intrigued right from the outset. Now, a film-maker must do exactly

Pip's first meeting with Magwitch. Finlay Currie and
Anthony Wager in GREAT EXPECTATIONS.

the same thing with a cinema audience, not always of course, by the same methods. People going to the theatre to see a play come at a specified time, sit down, the lights go down, up goes the curtain, and audiences in the theatre are prepared to listen. In the cinema, although audiences now make a point of arriving at the beginning rather than walking in at any time, as they used to do, it's a running battle with external factors. In England it's ice cream and advertisements, in America, pop corn, short subjects and cartoons. Sometimes I think cinemas do everything to destroy the atmosphere for the film that's about to appear, then down go the lights, and on comes your film; so I always do take particular trouble with the openings of my films, because I know that if I can get the interest of the audience in those first three minutes, I am half way there to holding them. Pip's first meeting with Magwitch, the convict, in the cemetery, seems to be remembered by everyone, I'm glad to say . . ."

Magwitch is captured as Pip looks on helplessly.

Comment

The praise that greeted *Brief Encounter* was great enough, but even greater was that which came to Lean for *Great Expectations.* This undoubtedly was his first masterpiece, even although he has surpassed himself several times since. The general feeling of satisfaction with *Great Expectations* is best summed up in the frequently stated observation that "what Olivier did for Shakespeare on the screen, Lean has done for Dickens." Just as the argument had always raged about Shakespeare's suitability to the film medium, so many scholars and purists believed that Dickens's long, rambling and massive works could not be filmed.

Today, it is enough that the film-maker conveys the spirit and intent of the author's original work, whether it is a novel, play or short story. In the Forties, the intelligentsia demanded a literary translation, which is of course, impossible, and if this was not produced, then the film was considered to be inferior. *Great Expectations* changed this attitude. It was so cleverly done that most moviegoers, who remembered the book, thought it was all in the film! The fact is that much of the narrative is missing and changes were made in time and place in order to give the film its shape and unity. But these were never damaging to Dickens or his characters.

By the time *Brief Encounter* was shown, the World War was over. Critics asked whether or not British film-makers, bereft of the impetus of war, could go on making films to excite the admiration of the world and place truth before simple fiction. It was a time to make another start. This was David Lean's (and Cineguild's) first break with Noël Coward. It was also the first time that David Lean and Ronald Neame had written their own screenplay. Previously, they had interpreted Coward plays in cinematic terms not by changes in his dialogue, characterisation and events but by stripping away their stage origins and making them works of the cinema. *Brief Encounter* is a splendid example of this. Yet it is fascinating to observe how different Lean's last film by Coward is from his first from Dickens. *Brief Encounter* had been expanded from a one-act play in the series "Tonight at 8.30" into a taut, controlled, unpretentious film of almost formal classical perfection, complete within itself.

Great Expectations is a marvelously controlled contraction of a sprawling romantic novel of incredible coincidences and misunderstandings, peopled by a gallery of characters so rich in detail, language and motivation that to bring them to life on film would be

John Mills as Pip, and Alec Guinness as Herbert Pocket
in a scene from GREAT EXPECTATIONS.

Valerie Hobson as Estella in a dramatic encounter with Pip.

a challenge and a despair to the most accomplished film-maker. How Lean and Neame achieved this, first in their screenplay, and then Lean in directing it, is an act of artistic creativity hard to describe. Lean will simply say that it was an intuitive knowledge of what would transfer well to the screen in cinematic terms. It was his visual mind at work again. He could see all its excitement and beauty in terms of cinema, keeping in mind that it was Dickens's work that would come to the screen, in words, spirit and social concern.

The result is a spell-binding picture rising to heights of poetry, imagination, sympathy, affection and love of mankind. Here is Lean the complete director at work, from the splendid control of the actors, all in the best Dickensian manner, the use of light and shade, sound and music, words and images. It is a constant procession of moving, charming, witty, lovely, despairing, sad and exciting events set against John Bryan's evocative creation of old London as we like to think it was from tales and drawings of the era, alternating with the desolate marshes, and the bleak inn with the squeaking sign. From Pip's opening encounter in the mist-shrouded churchyard with the convict, Magwitch, to the old man's death, this is a gripping and memorable film. No one will forget

Alec Guinness, Bernard Miles as Joe Gargary and John Mills in GREAT EXPECTATIONS.

Martita Hunt's Miss Havisham in her decaying yet still elegant mansion, her rich voice crying out her pain, and her revenge upon men. There is the lovely Jean Simmons as the young Estella and Anthony Wager as young Pip, both of whom grow up and are played by Valerie Hobson and John Mills, the latter in his third film with Lean and becoming more accomplished and sensitive with each performance. Bernard Miles as Joe Gargery, was playing in his second film with Lean. Alec Guinness, a new actor destined to become one of the few great character actors to achieve stardom, appears as Mr. Pocket. Finlay Currie, Francis L. Sullivan, O. B. Clarence, create memorable characters. Here is a gallery of great British players, to say nothing of great Dickensian figures all finely balanced in a film of sweeping drama and technical finesse, in which the robust exaggerations of Dickens in events and characterisation are carefully adjusted to the realism of the cinema. The dialogue is vivid and alive. It is one of the few times that a film of a novel creates the same compelling excitement the reader feels when first taking up the book. It is alive with the dark and melancholy beauty of English weather and the drab Medway Saltings.

Great Expectations was Lean's first postwar film. That it had nothing to do with the postwar problems which beset Britain after

A low camera angle accentuates the gothic interior of Miss Havisham's decaying mansion. Left to right: Mills, Hunt, Hobson.

Lean's close attention to detail gives a rich period flavour.
Valerie Hobson and John Mills in GREAT EXPECTATIONS.

peace had arrived was deliberate. There had been enough drabness, tragedy and heartache during the war years. Here was a
form of intelligent escapism rooted in British character, tradition
and literary achievement. It was like revisiting old friends, or discovering them anew. The moral of the piece is abundantly clear:
good manners and high breeding do not make human beings and
both Pip and Estella find themselves elegant and independent, but
still of the lower-middle class.

In scene after scene, David Lean shows his imaginative use of
film. Miss Havisham catches fire; Pip pulls off the rotting table
cloth, as it comes toward us, the camera moves swiftly over it; Miss
Havisham's screams are picked up and echoed in Walter Goehr's
beautiful score. At the public hanging, Pip looks out of the window;
there is silence; the crowd roars as the prisoners drop, the camera
moves up to Pip's face. In the scene where Pip meets Estella again
in the garden and they walk around, splendidly dressed, having
become snobs in acquiring class, Lean gives a sudden insight into
these people, a dismaying realisation that they are extremely fool-
ish, even worthless at this moment, just as in *Brief Encounter* in
the scene where Alec Harvey "humbly begs" Laura Jesson to ac-
company him, we see the absurdity of their behaviour and of their

A meticulous set typical of John Bryan's award-winning production design.

John Mills (left), and Francis L. Sullivan (right) as the lawyer Jaggers.

Miss Havisham (Martita Hunt) enthroned among the cobwebs.

Pip pulls off the rotting table cloth, undisturbed since Miss Havisham's wedding day. One of the film's outstanding sets.

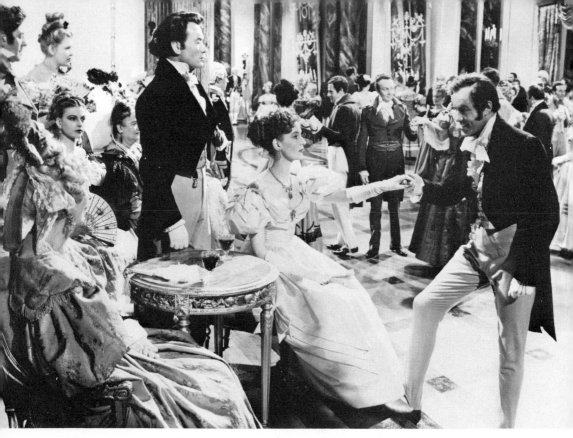

In the sumptuous ball scene, Pip displays his acquired class.

Now prosperous, Herbert Pocket and Pip drink a toast.

Magwitch's plan to escape by packet steamer is foiled.

attitude toward love. This raises another interesting point, and, whether David Lean sensed it at the time or not, he doesn't say, but many people feel that *Brief Encounter* seen today is dated, but no one thinks that *Great Expectations,* a picture which recreates the past, is dated, nor will it ever be because it is not about a period of time we have lived in and recognise. Would *Brief Encounter* seem more real and honest if it were filmed today as a story set in 1839? Can we only find truth and reality in hindsight, in recreating past eras or times in which few people remember what it was really like, and characters and events can be shaped into greater dramatic form? Whether Lean realised this, of the ten films he was to make following *Great Expectations* only three were to deal with immediately contemporary events.

Note: twenty-five years later, Ronald Neame directed a musical version of "A Christmas Carol" entitled *Scrooge,* with Albert Finney as Ebenezer Scrooge.

Oliver Twist (John Howard Davies) asks for more.

6. Oliver Twist (1948)

Director: David Lean. *Screenplay:* David Lean and Stanley Haynes, based on the book by Charles Dickens. *Photography:* Guy Green. *Camera Operator:* Oswald Morris. *Production design:* John Bryan. *Editor.* Jack Harris. *Costumes:* Margaret Furse. *Sound Recording:* Stanley Lambourne and Gordon K. McCullum. *Sound Editor:* Winston Ryder. *Make Up:* Stuart Freebourne. *Special Photographic Effects:* Joan Suttie and Stanley Grant. *Continuity:* Margaret Sibley. *Assistant Director:* George Pollock. *Music:* Sir Arnold Bax; solo pianoforte, Harriet Cohen, played by the Philharmonia Orchestra conducted by Muir Mathieson. *Producer:* Ronald Neame. *Production:* Cineguild, for the J. Arthur Rank Organisation. *Release:* Eagle-Lion, Odeon, Leicester Square, London. June 22, 1948. 10,436 ft. 116 minutes.

CAST

Bill Sikes	Robert Newton
Fagin	Alec Guinness
Nancy	Kay Walsh
Mr. Bumble	Francis L. Sullivan
Mr. Brownlow	Henry Stephenson

Mrs. Corney	Mary Clare
Oliver Twist	John Howard Davies
Oliver's Mother	Josephine Stuart
Police Official	Henry Edwards
Monks	Ralph Truman
The Artful Dodger	Anthony Newley
Singers at the "Three Cripples"	Hattie Jacques, Betty Paul
Workhouse Master	Kenneth Downy
Mr. Sowerberry	Gibb McLaughlin
Mrs. Sowerberry	Kathleen Harrison
Mrs. Bedwin	Amy Veness
Bookseller	W. G. Fay
Chief of Police	Maurice Denham
Mr. Grimwit	Frederick Lloyd
Chairman of the Board	Ivor Barnard
Mrs. Thingummy	Deidre Doyle
Annie	Edie Martin
Martha	Fay Middleton
Charlotte	Diana Dors
Noah Claypole	Michael Dear
Mr. Fang	Graveley Edwards
Landlord of the "Three Cripples"	Peter Bull
Charlie Bates	John Potter
Workhouse Doctor	Maurice Jones

Story

The birth of Oliver Twist, his life as a pauper boy in the parish workhouse, his flight from the house of Mr. Sowerberry, the undertaker, and his meeting in London with the Artful Dodger, his schooling under Fagin, his rescue from a life of thieving by the kindly Mr. Brownlow, his re-abduction by Fagin's gang, the murder of Nancy by Bill Sikes because of her attempt to restore Oliver to Mr. Brownlow, and the pursuit of Sikes by the police and the enraged mob, ending with Sikes's death and Oliver's final rescue— these are the incidents of Dickens's novel which in the main have been taken for the narrative of this film.

David Lean

"I tried throughout the writing and filming of both *Great Expectations* and *Oliver Twist* to recapture my impressions on first

Mr. Bumble (Francis L. Sullivan) leads Oliver past one of
John Bryan's impressively dour Dickensian sets.

Mr. Sowerberry (Gibb McLaughlin) and Mr. Bumble.
decide to buy Oliver after seeing his sale notice.

*Kay Walsh as Nancy, Alec Guinness heavily disguised as Fagin
and John Howard Davies in a scene from OLIVER.*

reading the two stories. I imagined *Great Expectations* as a fairy
tale, just not quite true, and *Oliver Twist* as a grimly realistic study
of what poverty was like at that time. In writing the script, we
read and re-read the novels and made a one-line summary of the
actual incidents in each chapter, ignoring all conversation and de-
scriptive matter. Any duplication or similarity of scenes was cut
out. Actual scenes for the film were built up from this summary.
Dickens's dialogue is perfect for the screen, and almost all of it was
taken straight from the book. Occasionally, an incident has been

*Bill Sikes (Robert Newton) introduces Oliver to a welcoming Fagin.
The Artful Dodger (Anthony Newley) and Nancy inspect the new arrival.*

altered to suit the demands of the cinema. In some cases, the actual
sequence of events has been interchanged to make for a better
balance and dramatic value. Technically I would say that *Oliver
Twist* was more difficult to adapt for the screen than *Great Expectations*. The main problem was that of making fantastic, larger than
life characters fit into a starkly real setting."

Comment

By now, David Lean was the most favoured and the most independent of all British directors. There was considerable disappointment on the part of many of his admirers that at a time when
Italian neo-realist directors were shooting significant films about
postwar problems, Lean should choose to remain in the past and
make a second film from Dickens, a film which it was said, failed
to further his distinguished career. Yet it was admitted that *Oliver
Twist* was a superbly made picture, the main criticism being that
it jollified Bumble, Fagin and Sikes. Looked at today and in com-
parison with Carol Reed's imaginative musical version of Lionel

Bart's *Oliver!* (1970) it is positively dark, gloomy and grim. Certainly the Americans didn't think it jollified Fagin. So many considered it to be anti-semitic that it received only limited showings in a cut version, and quickly disappeared from view. It is not even seen on television. Writing his screenplay (in co-operation this time with Stanley Haynes) Lean again made a fine transfiguration of the long and involved book into manageable film material. Oddly enough, while expressing reservations about the suitability of choice on Lean's part in filming *Oliver Twist*, few critics noted that with it the director went even further than *Great Expectations* in his technical and artistic explorations. His restless spirit of experimentation informs every sequence of this picture, the work of an artist who still seeks new ways to tell stories, new forms of narrative and visual expression; and this within the framework of an expensive film being made for a mass audience. Just as Pip's meeting with Magwitch in the wind-blown churchyard at the beginning of *Great Expectations* is film history, so too is the magnificent long opening of *Oliver Twist*, in which Oliver's mother struggles across the moors to the workhouse under a cloud streaked sky and in a fearsome thunder storm to give birth to Oliver and then to die in sackcloth and gloom. John Bryan's settings here are even more dark and stylised than his designs in *Great Expectations*, with more interior work. The spirit is properly darker and life more desperate and despairing. There is no coach and horses with trumpets sounding when Oliver goes to London as there was for Pip.

There is not as much class-consciousness about the characters in *Oliver Twist* as there is in *Great Expectations*, except that Oliver, quietly but spiritedly played by John Howard Davies, emerges from the workhouse speaking beautiful English (in spite of his association with boys from the lower classes) which indicates to us immediately that he must be related to someone of the upper class, and so it turns out to be when Mr. Brownlow discovers him and restores him to his true place in life.

All the casting and the performances are again exceptional. The three figures we all carry in our minds from childhood reading of the book are Sikes, Fagin and Bumble, and here Lean is working with actors who have been in his earlier films. Newton is a brooding, brutal Sikes; Francis L. Sullivan makes Bumble a bumbler, lacking the cruelty which Dickens saw in him, in his treatment of the orphaned children, and Alec Guinness as Fagin is unrecognisably brilliant and pathetic, a role which launched Guinness on a career of peculiar people in various disguises. Kay Walsh (so foully

Bill Sikes stands aghast having murdered Nancy.

murdered by Sikes), gives a fetching performance as Nancy, determined, sympathetic, yet loyal. Although many minor characters are missing in both *Great Expectations* and *Oliver Twist*, the audience feels they must be around somewhere in this crowded gallery, although it would have strengthened the narratives just to have them pass by, or say a few words. The camera can show in an instant what it takes a writer pages to describe: for instance, Noah Claypole kicking a stone out of jealousy when Oliver is dressed up to become a mourner.

The music, this time by Sir Arnold Bax, is one of the great film scores of the period, and gives splendid operatic overtones to this very operatic material. The chilling sets of Fagin's den overlooking Saint Paul's are a masterly design of chimney pots, rooftops, menacing shadows, smoke and spires.

Here is a mixture of dreams, legends, fairy tales and social criticism, and in this last respect, Lean has retained more of Dickens's anger and rage over the poverty of the people and their persecution than he did in *Great Expectations*. Yet perversely, he pays little attention to Fagin's "children" and their agony, and Anthony Newley's Artful Dodger is curiously muted. The ending seems a selfish one, happiness for Oliver, but no thought for the boys who are left behind.

It is interesting to study the depiction of the scenes of violence in both these Dickens pictures; in each case, where today we would have explicit depictions with much blood, here they all take place off-camera, and yet are all the more horrifying and more imaginatively shown: Sikes's dog scrabbling in panic at the door as Nancy is murdered, Sikes trying to drown the dog, Sikes falling from the roof.

The film abounds in Lean's superb use of images, rather than words, and his remarkable sound and editing are best illustrated in the famous "ask for more" sequence: the lots are drawn, the hands stretch out for the straws, there is a gasp as Oliver finds himself with the loser, the sound of the boys feet as they disappear leaving Oliver alone, his walk up the aisle, a small figure, rows of faces at the table, a sudden hush, the trembling request, a fast succession of astonished official faces ending in the notice going up "Boy for Sale £5," and Mr. Sowerberry intoning "I'll take him." For economy of expression, there are few sequences in any film as effective and inspiring as this.

Sikes kidnaps Oliver as a hostage in his attempt to escape.

**A torch carrying crowd watch Sikes and Oliver on the roof tops,
just before Sikes falls and hangs himself.**

Ann Todd as Mary and Trevor Howard as Steven Stratton
her old lover meet again in Switzerland.

7. The Passionate Friends (1949)

Director: David Lean. *Screenplay:* Eric Ambler, adapted by Lean and Stanley Haynes from the novel by H. G. Wells. *Photography:* Guy Green. *Camera Operator:* Oswald Morris. *Production design:* John Bryan. *Assistant Art Director:* T. Hopewell-Ashe. *Editor:* Geoffrey Foot. *Sound Recording:* Stanley Lambourne and Gordon K. McCallum. *Sound Editor:* Winston Ryder. *Music:* Richard Addinsell. *Assistant Director:* George Pollock. *Producer:* Ronald Neame. *Production:* Cineguild for the J. Arthur Rank Organisation. *Release:* General Film Distributors (GFD). Odeon, Leicester Square, London. January 26, 1949. 8,154 ft. 91 minutes. (US title: *One Woman's Story*)

CAST

Mary	Ann Todd
Howard Justin	Claude Rains
Steven Stratton	Trevor Howard
Pat	Isabel Dean
Miss Layton	Betty Ann Davies
Servant	Arthur Howard
Hotel Manager	Guido Lorraine

Hall Porter   Marcel Poncin
Chambermaid   Natasha Sokolova
Flowerwoman   Helen Burls
Emigration Official   Jean Serett
Charwoman   Frances Waring
Bridge Guest   Wanda Rogerson
Solicitor   Wilfred Hyde-White

Story

Mary Justin meets an old love, Steven Stratton, at the Chelsea Arts Ball, and though securely and placidly married to the kind and detached Howard Justin, falls in love with Steven once again. Torn between real love and security, Mary decides to remain with her husband, who is willing to forgive on the understanding that she and Steven do not meet again. Nine years later, Mary and Steven, who is now happily married, find themselves in the same hotel in the Swiss mountains. While Mary is waiting for Howard to return from a business trip they spend one day together. Justin returns before he is expected, witnesses their parting and immediately puts

Ann Todd and Claude Rains, who plays Howard Justin, her possessive husband, dressed for the ball.

*Trevor Howard and Ann Todd in a scene
from THE PASSIONATE FRIENDS.*

the worst construction possible on the meeting. Circumstantial evidence is against them, and Justin institutes divorce proceedings. Mary, unable to cope with the situation, attempts suicide on the London underground, but her husband, realising at last that he does love his wife, rescues her from death.

David Lean

"I like this subject. I find it very appealing. It's an intimate love story and has a lot of *Brief Encounter* in it. But instead of a suburban railway station, it has a more glamorous setting, or at least, one which many audiences tend to think of as being glamorous. I like making films about women, I like telling love stories, I think they are fascinating. I think the excitement of a love affair is hard to match. This story is about temptation. It's much removed from the original novel, but the spirit is there. Adapting it called for a different approach to the one we used for *Great Expectations* and *Oliver Twist*. People who hadn't read these books for some time thought they were seeing the books. In fact they weren't; they were seeing an 'impression' of the book. It was a realistic, visual

*Lean's lyrical and dazzlingly photographed landscapes act
as a back-drop to the lovers Howard and Todd.*

impression. It had to be because the books were so well known, and had audiences not recognised them, we would have disappointed them and they in turn would consider that we had adapted them badly. The book we worked from with this picture was not so well known. This gave us more freedom to experiment with it."

Comment

Mary (Ann Todd) is on her way to Switzerland. The time is contemporary with the film, 1948. She is to meet her husband. Who should be staying in the next room in their hotel but her former lover! After an innocent day together, she is confronted by her husband, who says he will divorce her. We find out why through an elaborate flashback to nine years earlier, and then into another flashback within the flashback, to five years previous to this. Based on a novel by H. G. Wells concerning the advantages of free love, with a Boer War background, Eric Ambler's screenplay would seem to indicate that it was closer to Noël Coward's Brief Encounter than to H. G. Wells's story. For David Lean, it seems at first a clear case of repetition; here are the flashbacks, the lovers (the man is once more a doctor), the attempted suicide under a train, the return to the husband. But it is only superficially similar. Mary and Steven have been lovers before her marriage. She abandoned Steven for the wealth and security of her banker husband, and gave up love at the same time. Their brief encounter takes place five years later, her husband forgives on the understanding that it ends. The final innocent meeting is the one which breaks down (at last) the frigidity which had existed on the part of the husband toward his wife. The triangle here is complete. The important difference between the two films however, is one of circumstance. Tired perhaps with Dickensian gloom and working and middle class existence, Lean here took his first small step into the internationalisation of cinema, into sophisticated society, exotic backgrounds, fashionable people who are free of all restraint. While Brief Encounter was drabness and tea-shop chatter, The Passionate Friends brought glamour into British cinema in a way the American studios might have envied. The public, which stayed away from Brief Encounter on the grounds that they had seen enough of railway stations, tea-shops and their own homes, was more inclined to see Ann Todd, beautifully dressed, shining with radiance, holidaying in Switzerland, and never aging. The people in the cinema in Brief Encounter watching "Flames of Passion" (the fictitious movie playing there) are the same people

*Mary and Steven spend an innocent day
before the return of her husband.*

who would prefer to see *The Passionate Friends* rather than *Brief Encounter*.

The acting performances by the three principal players are masterly, particularly Claude Rains, who looks down with superiority and scorn on lovers, never having experienced the emotion himself. Technically, David Lean has pursued his intentions once again to the limit, resulting in a dazzlingly photographed, fast moving, sharp, incisive and delicate study of tangled emotions, loneliness and longing. While the characters are not exactly warm or attractive, their feelings are tensely conveyed in this lyrical study set in white Alpine sunshine and snow. There is guilt here too, but not humiliation. However, it is not the uncertain Mary Justin who will be remembered by audiences but the genuine Laura Jesson.

Howard Justin saves his wife from suicide on the London underground, and is finally reconciled to her.

*Madeleine Smith (Ann Todd) is embraced by Emile L'Angelier,
(Ivan Desny) whom she is later accused of murdering.*

8. Madeleine (1950)

Director: David Lean. *Screenplay:* Stanley Haynes and Nicholas Phipps. *Photography:* Guy Green. *Sets:* John Bryan. *Costumes:* Margaret Furse. *Editor:* Geoffrey Foot. *Production Manager:* Norman Spencer. *Assistant Director:* George Pollock. *Music:* William Alwyn. *Producer:* Stanley Haynes. *Production:* A David Lean film for Cineguild. *Release:* GFD (UK), UA (USA). Odeon, Leicester Square, London. February 14, 1950. 10,289 ft. 114 minutes.

CAST

Madeleine Smith	Ann Todd
Emile L'Angelier	Ivan Desny
Mr. Minnoch	Norman Wooland
Mr. Smith	Leslie Banks
Mrs. Smith	Barbara Everest
Janet Smith	Susan Stranks
Bessie Smith	Patricia Raine
Christina	Elizabeth Sellars
Dr. Thompson	Edward Chapman
Mrs. Jenkins	Jean Cadell

Mr. Thuau	Eugene Deckers
Mr. Murdoch	Ivor Barnard
Lord Advocate	Barry Jones
Lord Justice	David Morne
Clerk of the Court	Henry Edwards
Dean of Faculty	Andre Morell
Dr. Penny	Kynaston Reeves
Dr. Yeoman	Cameron Hall
William (Boot Boy)	Douglas Barr
Mrs. Grant (Woman at Ball)	Irene Brown
Highland Dancers	Alfred Rodriguez, Moira Fraser

Story

Madeleine, beautiful, quietly passionate, enigmatic daughter of Mr. Smith, a prosperous and very Victorian Glasgow merchant, has an infatuation for Emile L'Angelier, a handsome but poor and not-too-scrupulous Frenchman. The two meet secretly at night in the basement of Madeleine's home. Mr. Smith wants Madeleine to marry Mr. Minnoch, one of her own circle, and is annoyed when Madeleine keeps refusing to agree. Meanwhile, Emile becomes

A confrontation between Madeleine and her strictly Victorian father (Leslie Banks).

*L'Angelier and Madeleine in a tense encounter
as their relationship deteriorates.*

L'Angelier watches Madeleine dancing with Mr. Minnoch (Norman Wooland) at the ball.

jealous and threatens to show Madeleine's letters to her father unless she introduces him to her family. Emile refuses Madeleine's pleas to take her away, so they might marry and live elsewhere. Soon afterwards, Emile dies of arsenic poisoning and Madeleine is arrested and charged with murder. Despite the strong evidence against her, her counsel puts up such a brilliant defence that the jury returns the Scottish "not proven" verdict. Madeleine does not go into the box, and the audience is left in the same doubt as the jury.

David Lean

"Here I think we had another first-rate love story, only this time we worked from life, the actual story of Madeleine Smith, which we re-created from news stories and court records. This was hard to do because no one but Madeleine Smith really knew what happened at certain moments in her association with her lover, and we had to be very careful not to show anything happening which was not in accord with what was brought out in the trial. Yet, at the same time, we had to leave audiences with the same element

*Lean emphasises the fatal bottle of poison,
set here between Madeleine and Mr. Murdoch (Ivor Barnard).*

of doubt as to what actually happened as was found by the jury. And in what way was Madeleine to be portrayed? She must have been a passionate woman by all accounts, also somewhat enigmatic. I think we got a good dramatic structure out of her story, and I think it was very original, very romantic and not a little sad."

Comment

Madeleine begins with the Smith family's arrival at 7, Blythswood Square, Glasgow, and ends with Madeleine leaving the courthouse, a free woman. In between, Lean, Haynes and Phipps have constructed an ingenious screenplay remaining faithful to all known facts. Just as no one really knew whether or not Madeleine Smith poisoned her lover, the film makes no attempt to come to a decision, leaving the question open. Miss Smith never spoke of it again during the rest of her life, and she carried her secret, if there was one, to her grave, as the saying goes.

This is a clever film, carefully thought out, constructed and acted. Once again, Lean is concerned with the excitement of passion and love under forbidden circumstances. In the role of Madeleine, Ann

Arresting use of the wide-angle lens, with Madeleine's veil heightening the tragic element in the trial scene.

Todd's somewhat glacial and enigmatic manner seems ideally suited to the character of this strange, calm, self-possessed girl. The wildness and passion attributed to her are visually illustrated by Lean in the scene where she meets her lover outside her family's country home. It is night time, they are in the hills overlooking the Clyde, a dance is in progress down in the village. The strains of the music drift up to them and slowly she begins to dance, finally persuading her lover to join her, the sequence ending with her seduction. This is naturally not shown, due to censorship at that time. But no more needs to be seen, just as in the sequence where, back home, she admits L'Angelier and asks him for her letters. He refuses and she falls to the floor crying. He stands over her, she looks up at him, we know what will take place, for Lean has created simply by glances, close-ups, and movements, an atmosphere of intense sexuality.

The court scene is masterly in its depiction of the trial and here Lean uses his flashback technique with great skill. The prosecution witnesses make their appearance, and then when Andre Morell, who delivers the defence (taken from the court record) with tremendous passion and eloquence, is summing up, other witnesses are shown in brief flashbacks. John Bryan's settings of Victorian Glasgow including a faithful exterior of 7, Blythswood Square, are extremely evocative and authentic, and the entire cast is faultless.

It speaks much for David Lean's skill that while an audience knows the outcome of *Madeleine*, he creates an excitement and tension, and a concern for the characters which is so compelling that at times it becomes unbearable. Visually, and in human terms, Lean makes every moment count, and again uses the weather, the drab surroundings, the suffocating class consciousness of the Smiths, to great effect. This fascinating criminal riddle was brought to life with intelligence and understanding, and was the last of the Cineguild films.

The defence lawyer (Andre Morell) conducts
a cross examination in the masterly court scene.

Nigel Patrick as Tony Garthwaite, with a symbol of his obsession with speed.

9. The Sound Barrier (1952)

Director: David Lean. *Screenplay:* Terence Rattigan. *Photography:* Jack Hildyard. *Aerial unit director:* Anthony Squire. *Aerial Unit Cameramen:* John Wilcox, Jo Jago, Peter Newbrook. *Editor:* Geoffrey Foot. *Set Design:* Vincent Korda. *Art Directors:* Joseph Bato, John Hawkesworth. *Music:* Malcolm Arnold. *Producer:* David Lean. *Associate Producer:* Norman Spencer. *Production:* London Films. *Release:* British Lion. Carlton Cinema, London. July 22, 1952. 10,475 ft. 118 minutes. (US title: *Breaking the Sound Barrier*)

CAST

John Ridgefield	Ralph Richardson
Susan Garthwaite	Ann Todd
Tony Garthwaite	Nigel Patrick
Philip Peel	John Justin
Jess Peel	Dinah Sheridan
Will Sparks	Joseph Tomelty
Christopher Ridgefield	Denholm Elliott
Windy Williams	Jack Allen
Fletcher	Ralph Michael
ATA Officer	Donald Harron

Story

During the War, WAAF officer Susan Ridgefield, the daughter of a wealthy, self-made owner of an aircraft manufacturing company, marries Tony Garthwaite, a young fighter pilot. She takes him home to meet her family. Susan's brother, Christopher, afraid of his domineering father and desperately anxious to please him, is about to make his first solo flight; he loses his nerve, crashes and is killed. Susan blames her father for her brother's death, but after the war, Tony accepts the father's offer of a job as a test pilot for the new jet airplane being developed. He and Susan go to live at the father's home. Tony, enthusiastic, but not particularly intelligent, is soon on friendly terms with Ridgefield, though Susan's relations with her father become increasingly strained. She tries to dissuade Tony from testing the new jet plane which Ridgefield hopes will be the first to fly faster than sound. She fails, and in the final test the aircraft disintegrates when it reaches the speed of sound. Susan, horrified by her father's apparent indifference to Tony's death, goes to the home of another pilot, Philip Peel, and his wife, where her baby is born. To the bewilderment of the daughter, who cannot understand how, or for what, her father is ready to take such risks with lives, Ridgefield asks Philip to test the rebuilt aircraft. He succeeds in breaking through the sound barrier. Susan discovers that her father is less ruthlessly single-minded than he appears, and decides to return home with her child.

David Lean

"We filmed the opening flying sequence as a prologue to the credits for a very special reason, because round about the time we were doing the script, several people said that nobody would understand what the sound barrier was, so we thought we'd open the film on an incident that actually took place during the war. A pilot was feeling very gay one day, and he put his Spitfire into a flat out dive, and he went faster and faster, and suddenly the machine started to shake, and he pulled on the stick to correct it, and the harder he pulled, the more the nose went down, until he finally throttled back and pulled out of the dive. Now the aeroplane had been shaking madly, and he didn't know quite what had happened. In fact, he had touched the edge, as it were, of the sound barrier, and we show this as the opening of the film, then follow it with the title 'Sound Barrier,' so the first sequence describes what the

Tony Garthwaite and Susan Garthwaite (Ann Todd)
as a happily married young couple.

John Ridgefield (Ralph Richardson) demonstrates a new light-weight
metal to the Garthwaite's and his son Christopher (Denholm Elliott).

An anxious moment from THE SOUND BARRIER;
Ralph Richardson, Ann Todd and Nigel Patrick.

film is about. We have seen trips to the moon and very exciting they are, and we have also seen a lot of films about wartime flying, but in between wartime flying and these science fiction films is another tremendous story, or at least so I thought, in the development of this new jet aeroplane. That's really why I did it, and because I thought very few people knew the reality of it was more exciting perhaps than the fiction.

"I like flying, but I've only been a passenger in an airliner. I have always admired the beauty of flying, and I wanted to get some of that into the film. Later on, I made a flight in a jet plane and then I was absolutely certain there was a story to be written. I spent about a year going to aircraft factories and talking to pilots because it is a very complicated subject. One of the chief difficulties, I think, was that all the flying people were worried that I was going to do a great big melodrama, that I'd overdo it; then after a short time they saw that I was serious about it, and they were of tremendous help. De Havillands gave a great deal of help. I spent a couple of weekends up at Rolls Royce. The more I saw, the keener I became on the subject. This was all before we started to write it. Although we had a dramatic story we really had no story at all, we had a mass of background material. We went to Terence Rattigan and asked him to write the script because he was a first-rate writer of characters. We thought, "who better than Rattigan?" And he also is one of the very, very few people capable of writing an original screen story, which in fact he did on this occasion."

Comment

In the two years which elapsed between the showing of *Madeleine* and *The Sound Barrier,* great changes were taking place in British film-making—an era was ending and a new, uncertain period beginning. In brief, the Rank Organisation, which had done so much to encourage and support British films since the early years of the war, found itself with enormous losses. These were due in part to its own poor judgement, but also as a result of bungling by the British government. In an attempt to solve the postwar monetary crisis, it placed an enormous tax on American films (which were draining the country of valuable dollar reserves). The Americans retaliated by withholding all films from the British market. The Rank Organisation (and other studios) tried to fill the vacuum by increasing production in a hurry, the result being a number of mediocre pictures rushed out to meet an emergency. And no sooner were these films on the market than the tax was rescinded, American films flooded into the country, and the make-do British pictures represented a lost investment. As well as this, many of the films made by the independent producers working under the Rank banner had cost too much, could not recover their costs in the UK, and had failed to make any impact on the much-needed, valuable American market.

All of a sudden, that marvellous period of discovery and excitement that had begun about the same time that Lean's *In Which We Serve* was made, and that had yielded so many likeable, genuine and remarkable British films, players and directors, was over. The pleasure of discovery by the British people of themselves on the screen during the difficult years of warfare had rightfully become, for the most part, a regular part of their lives, and, like all art and entertainment, new faces, new voices, and new explorations were expected and demanded by another generation coming of age. On top of all this was the Government's decision to replace the tax on American films with a withholding arrangement, under which the Americans were asked to leave a large percentage of their earnings in London as assets, not to be taken out of the country. To

A determined looking John Ridgefield is confronted by his daughter.

The newspaper headline presages disaster for
Tony Garthwaite: Ann Todd, Trevor Howard.

make use of this money and make (hopefully) profits from it, the American studios, which were themselves undergoing great crisis in Los Angeles due to the competition of television and changing public tastes in entertainment, took advantage of the then lower production costs in Britain to use this money to make films. This, together with the advantages of the Production Fund, resulted in the gradual withdrawal of British money for production, to be replaced by American money, and although most of the directors, writers, technicians and stars in the films were British, the American control (which lasted until 1969) was noticeable, and British pictures (there was considerable argument as to whether they could even be called British any longer) took on a different character, a different look, pace, style and content. Soon the Ealing comedies, the Gainsborough melodramas, Group Three productions, the Archers, Wessex Films, Two Cities, Individual Films, Sydney Box Productions, Eagle-Lion Distributors, would be gone, and with them, Cineguild.

For David Lean it was the close of his long partnership with Ronald Neame, Anthony Havelock-Allan, Guy Green, George Pollock, Stanley Haynes, John Bryan, Oswald Morris, and many unit technicians. Neame, Green and Pollack all became directors themselves. It was a period of indecision and retrenchment for most film-makers, but Lean's reputation, "the most individual and brilliant director in the country," was not to be lost on producers. Although the Rank Organisation had received most of the limelight during the Forties and Fifties, one of Britain's most famous prewar producers, Sir Alexander Korda, had continued to make distinguished films during the postwar years, under his established and respected London Films trademark. Also working for Korda was the accomplished Sir Carol Reed.

When the Cineguild team parted company, Korda invited David Lean to work with him. The result was *The Sound Barrier*. Again, for David Lean, this was the first step toward independent film-making. It is, of course, impossible for a director to make a film by himself, but what is meant by this is that he no longer had any partners, associates or friends to consider. He became the individual film-maker, an artist without associations, whose stature and strength was to become almost legendary. No director is ever completely free as long as he must work with a producer, who has usually raised the money, and therefore expects to have some say in the way the film is completed. Lean had to work with producers in the years to come, but for the most part he was also his own

Tony Garthwaite visits the production hanger.

producer or worked jointly with a producer. His strength and determination, which are formidable, were to carry him through enormous pressures and opposing point of view. When he moved to Shepperton Studios for Korda, David Lean was taking the first steps into a new period of achievement.

The Sound Barrier proved to be an amazingly prophetic picture. Made at a time when the world was on the threshold of air travel by jet propelled aircraft, and when the problems of breaking the sound barrier with either military or civilian supersonic planes was thought to be as remote as reaching the moon, the subsequent opposition to the Concorde on the grounds of pollution and damage to nerves, hearing and property, are all suggested in this perceptive film. The whole concept of supersonic flying, as envisaged by Ridgefield, the aircraft builder, is "an evil vision," in the words of his daughter. Written by Terence Rattigan, there is far more "argument" in this narrative than in any other film made by Lean, revolving around the morality of Ridgefield's views and actions. The question then, as it is today, is the justification for pressing on with experiments into the unknown in which men's lives are at stake, for the dubious scientific benefits which might result from

Ann Todd and Nigel Patrick in a scene from THE SOUND BARRIER.

such experiments. The answer remains the same: that as long as there is an unknown and man thinks he has found a way of mastering another aspect of it, he will continue to experiment no matter how useless and expensive it may be. Dramatic conflict is provided in the opposition by Ridgefield's daughter to her father's "insane" ideas, which result in the death of his son and his son-in-law as they try out their aircraft at supersonic speeds. The father's theories are proved to be practical and the reconciliation between father and daughter, which might not seem entirely believable, comes about quite convincingly.

Physical drama is inherent in the exciting flying sequences which are beautifully photographed and edited (Lean is here working with Jack Hildyard, camera, and Geoffrey Foot, editor, the latter being the only person from the previous film to be with Lean), and once again the director has conceived a memorable opening scene: a Spitfire flying through the clouds, going into a dive and then, mysteriously, plunging out of control. Throughout, Malcolm Arnold's score is a symphony of sounds and music, dedicated, like the picture, to the mystique of flying. Ralph Richardson gives a clever, well-modulated performance as the determined aircraft builder. His breakdown on the fulfilment of his ambitions is one of his greatest acting moments. Ann Todd's role suggests depth of concern, while remaining outwardly reserved. Nigel Patrick makes a welcome contrast, with his casual, cheerful, irrelevant role, to the usual reserved Englishman. In his performance may be found the first indications of British character actors moving toward more outwardly expressive naturalism, in contrast to "old school tie" reserve. In making an ambitious, exploratory, picture such as this, David Lean brought himself into the present with impressive results, but many audiences failed to relate to the film and its problems as supersonic flying had little to do with the urgencies and realities of their own lives. The picture was neither out-right science fiction escapism, nor a subject vital to Britain's survival. While such experiments were taking place, and adding immeasurably to British knowledge of aircraft design and manufacture, few people identified with the subject and its questions of morality. Its appeal is greater today, its validity more apparent.

Ann Todd as Susan Garthwaite is finally reconciled to her father played by Ralph Richardson.

10. Hobson's Choice (1954)

Director: David Lean. *Screenplay:* Lean, Norman Spencer, and Wynyard Browne, from the play by Harold Brighouse. *Photography:* Jack Hildyard. *Camera Operator:* Peter Newbrook. *Editor:* Peter Taylor. *Art Director:* Wilfred Shingleton. *Sound Supervision:* John Cox. *Sound Recording:* Buster Ambler and Red Law. *Costume Design:* John Armstrong. *Music:* Malcolm Arnold. *Assistant Director:* Adrian Pryce-Jones. *Producer:* David Lean. *Associate Producer:* Norman Spencer. *Production:* London Films. *Release:* British Lion. Plaza Theatre, London. February 24, 1954. 9,675 ft. 107 minutes.

CAST

Hobson	Charles Laughton
Willie Mossop	John Mills
Maggie Hobson	Brenda de Banzie
Alice Hobson	Daphne Anderson
Vicky Hobson	Prunella Scales
Albert Prosser	Richard Wattis
Freddy Beenstock	Derek Bloomfield
Mrs. Hepworth	Helen Haye

Jim Heeler	Joseph Tomelty
Sam Minns	Julian Mitchell
Tudsbury	Gibb McLaughlin
Denton	Philip Stainton
Ada Figgins	Dorothy Gordon
Mrs. Figgins	Madge Brindley
Dr. McFarlane	John Laurie
Pat Beenstock	Raymond Huntley
Tubby Wadlow	Jack Howarth
Printer	Herbert C. Wanton

Story

Henry Horatio Hobson, owner of a well-established boot shop in Salford, Lancashire, has three motherless daughters. Hobson spends much of his time at the local pub with fellow tradesmen, and leaves the highly efficient and wily Maggie to run his home and business. Alice and Vicky are pursued by Albert Prosser and Freddie Beenstock, neighbours, but Hobson, a self-important but ineffectual domestic tyrant, refuses them settlements. When Mrs. Hepworth, a wealthy and influential customer, praises the craft of

Brenda de Banzie, Charles Laughton, Prunella Scales, Daphne Anderson and John Mills in a shot from HOBSON'S CHOICE.

John Mills as Willie Mossop.

Willie Mossup, Hobson's unlettered workman, Maggie, tired of being on the shelf, decides to marry Willie and set him up in opposition to her father. One night, Hobson, gloriously tight, falls into the cellar of his enemy, the town's pussyfoot, and is sued for trespass. Maggie intervenes and, with the help of Albert and Freddie, artfully secures, a sum that not only settles the action, but provides the girls with dowries. Hobson starts drinking in earnest and eventually becomes seriously ill. Maggie then brings off her final coup: she agrees to return home on her own terms—a full partnership in the business for her husband. Hobson accepts his daughter's ultimatum.

David Lean

"Most of the time, directing actors is a matter of gentle suppression and gentle encouragement. This was certainly true of Laughton, a remarkable artist. In the first two weeks of filming, I can get a good idea of the actors' requirements. Acting is a frightening job. It's their face on the screen, and in the beginning they can be worried, and frightened. I always keep at a slight distance from

Brenda de Banzie as Maggie Hobson, and John Mills as her husband in HOBSON'S CHOICE.

A gloriously drunk Hobson (Charles Laughton), totters homewards . . .

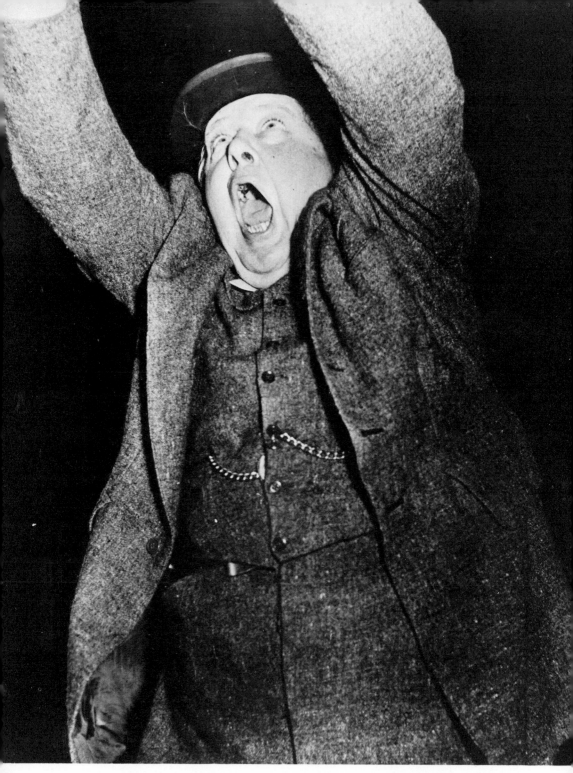

. . . *but comes to grief.*

the actors in every film, because if I get too chummy it's difficult to instruct them on the set and expect to be obeyed. I must have complete control, even if I have to sacrifice close friendships within the profession to maintain such control. It's all part of the job. Different actors call for different working methods. Some need a lot of encouragement. I haven't known a good actress or actor who didn't have tremendous nerves. Part of my job is to soothe those nerves and give them confidence. Some of them will become much too quiet and nervous and they must be 'pulled up.' Others will try to overcome their nerves by over-doing the part. They have to be 'pulled down,' and restrained. My job is to make the best use of their talents, and there are various ways of doing it with different actors."

Comment

With this play by Harold Brighouse, David Lean goes back into the past, forty years or more, not far enough away to be period comedy-drama, still near enough for the entire enterprise to seem dated or "old-fashioned." However much this provincial piece of domestic-relations repertory might seem to be shopworn, Lean was

Maggie demonstrates her managing ability
while Willie opts for discretion.

too skilful to allow it to sink into the same mediocrity that gave it life. It is first a show piece for the actor who plays Hobson, the truculent, pompous father, played here by Charles Laughton (returning home from America for the first time since the war ended) but who is almost eclipsed by the bright and brilliant playing of Brenda de Banzie as Maggie, the resolute daughter. Interestingly enough, Laughton, who was later to play *King Lear* at Stratford, interprets his role in such a way that many critics referred to his Hobson as a "King Lear figure" complete with his three daughters. Laughton could over-act with ease, and Lean seems to have had some difficulty keeping him under control here; but it's an immensely enjoyable human performance, played with gusto, of a man both ruminating and rascally, a different but just as tyrannical father as Leslie Banks's portrayal of Mr. Smith in *Madeleine*, and Ralph Richardson's role in *The Sound Barrier*. In the case of Hobson, however, he is deservedly defeated by his children. Miss de Banzie's performance is the best she ever gave in the cinema, and, regretfully, she never received any opportunities to do as well again. John Mills, in his fourth film with Lean, plays the simple, timid Mossop with easy charm and quiet humour.

The film is attractively made, a comedy-drama from Lancashire life and manners, close to the characters and their time, larger than life perhaps, as in Dickens, but still recognisable as natural and determined people. Lean again turned a play into a fine piece of cinema, with perfect settings, and the highlight remaining in the memories of most audiences, is that of Hobson's drunken pursuit of the moon's reflection through a number of puddles on his way home from the pub. This was David Lean's last black-and-white film.

Derek Bloomfield, Richard Wattis, Brenda de Banzie,
John Mills and Charles Laughton in HOBSON'S CHOICE.

Hobson resignedly accepts Mossop as his partner in the business.

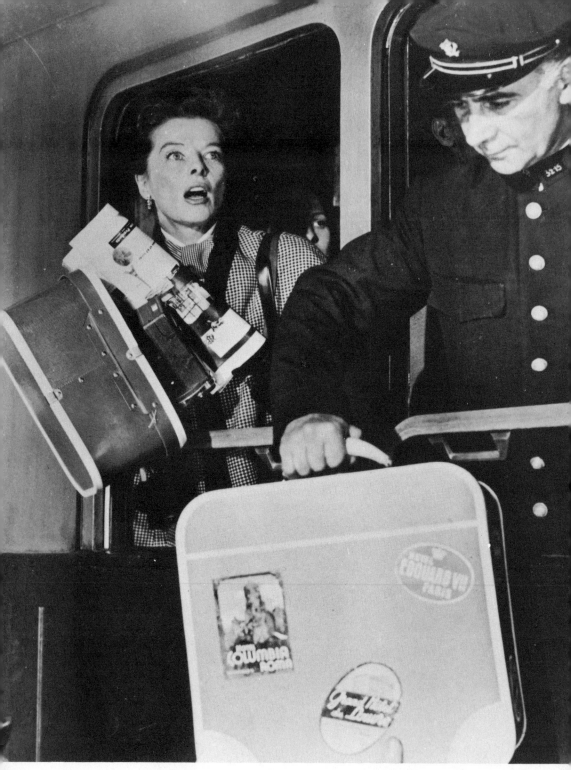

*Katharine Hepburn plays Jane Hudson, a middle-aged
American tourist in* SUMMER MADNESS.

11. Summer Madness (1955)

Director: David Lean. *Screenplay:* Lean and H. E. Bates, from the play, "The Time of the Cuckoo" by Arthur Laurents. *Photography:* Jack Hildyard (Eastmancolor, print by Technicolor). *Production design:* Vincent Korda. *Editor:* Peter Taylor. *Sound Recording:* Peter Handford. *Sound Re-recording:* John Cox. *Music:* Alessandro Cicognini. *Producer:* Ilya Lopert. *Associate Producer:* Norman Spencer. *Production:* A David Lean Production for London Films in association with Lopert Film Production. *Release:* US: United Artists. UK: Independent in association with British Lion. First shown in Venice May 29, 1955. 9,035 ft. 100 minutes. (US title: *Summertime*)

CAST

Jane Hudson	Katharine Hepburn
Renato Di Rossi	Rossano Brazzi
Signora Fiorini	Isa Miranda
Eddie Jaeger	Darren McGavin
Phyllis Jaeger	Mari Aldon
Mrs. McIlhenny	Jane Rose

Mr. McIlhenny	Macdonald Parke
Mauro	Gaitano Audiero
Englishman	Andre Morell
Vito	Jeremy Spenser
Giovanna	Virginia Simeon

Story

Jane Hudson, a middle-aged private secretary from Akron, Ohio, comes to Venice as a tourist on her first holiday in Europe. Determined to enjoy herself, she yet finds loneliness weighing on her in this romantically beautiful city. She tries to attach herself to other American visitors, strikes up a friendship with a little street urchin, and roams the city with her cine-camera; but still becomes only increasingly aware of her own essential isolation and insecurity. She doesn't approve when Signora Fiorina, owner of the *pensione* where she is staying, suggests she seek male companionship. Later, she is flustered by the appraising stare of a middle-aged Italian sitting at the next table at a café in the Piazza San Marco, and she hurriedly retreats. Next day, she again encounters the man, Renato Di Rossi, when she goes by chance into his antique shop. He is obviously attracted to her, and Jane finds herself romantically in love. She is distressed and shocked to discover that Renato is married and the father of several children, but she later surrenders: the relationship may not be the ideal romantic encounter she has imagined, but it is a real one. After a few idyllic days on one of the islands near Venice, her scruples and conscience are reawakened. Aware that the affair can only end unhappily, Jane renounces Renato and leaves Venice.

David Lean

"This was my first important location picture away from England, and I was tremendously excited and not a little worried. I'll tell you something interesting and odd about shooting location pictures. Because you are there, it's very easy to forget to shoot the long shots. Now that sounds unbelievable but I've known it to happen many times when I was a cutter. The film-maker goes out on a beach, shall we say, and he sees this huge beach and photographs the various shots he needs with the actors, or without them, and he forgets the camera hasn't photographed what he has been seeing all day! I like *Summer Madness* more than any other film I've done, I think, and working with Katharine Hepburn was a revelation of professionalism in action. I found her extremely exciting. As a result of making this film in Venice, I came to like Venice so much I have spent most of my spare time living there."

Comment

This film takes David Lean one more step towards becoming an international film-maker. At this time London Films found itself in financial difficulties. In an attempt to find a way out, it entered into a co-production arrangement for this film with Lopert Film Productions, associated with United Artists, to be filmed entirely

Jane Hudson wanders alone through Venice.

in Venice. For the first time (with the exception of the brief Swiss locations in *The Passionate Friends*) David Lean moved out of England to work on location. From now on, this became his way of life. For the first time he was working on a story and subject not British, from a play by an American writer, about an American woman on holiday in Venice. Although he had written the screenplay with H. E. Bates, and his unit was largely British, this was in effect his break with film-making in Britain, and the filming of British themes. Although all but one of his future productions concerns British characters and situations, they all take place as part of the international scene, with international players in exotic places. There are to be no more small-picture, black-and-white studies of home life.

This picture confirmed several patterns and themes characteristic of Lean's work, in both major and minor forms. It was the third variation of the *Brief Encounter* situation, and the fourth study of love, loneliness and passion, and the danger of infidelity and forbidden love. Once again, trains play a part in bringing the protagonists together, as they did in *Brief Encounter*. When Michael Wilding said goodbye to his *fiancée* from a train window in *In*

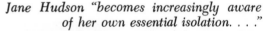

Jane Hudson "becomes increasingly aware of her own essential isolation. . . ."

Which We Serve, this was the beginning of Lean's fascination with trains, which appear in every major picture. Venice has never been photographed before or since with such an understanding of love and the expression of the excitement on first discovery, its sadness and remoteness when viewed from a lonely perspective. The story of the spinster from the new world visiting the old world and finding momentary enchantment at seeing what she has read about for such a long time in historic and romantic literature, of her seduction by a European lover, of her disillusionment and return to America with only a memory to comfort her and time to lessen sadness and guilt, is such a trite and well-known part of film and literature that it has become a joke, with every single woman tourist travelling alone in Europe being looked upon as fair game by the hordes of Europeans who live off the tourist economy. Fortunately, the changing social order is bringing it to an end, because travelling has become so much easier for the young and the relatively poor. The middle-aged spinsters of the Fifties who had finally saved up enough money to take the European holiday they had promised themselves for years and who had been reared in strict, puritanical homes which forbade sex out of wedlock, have

Katharine Hepburn against the beautiful Venetian location, strikes up an acquaintance with a street urchin.

Renato Di Rossi (Rossano Brazzi) admires Jane Hudson at a wayside café.

*The two become lovers, and in this scene spend
a few idyllic days on an island near Venice.*

*Katharine Hepburn and Rossano Brazzi in a
night club scene from SUMMER MADNESS.*

*In this long shot Lean lets Saint Mark's Square dwarf
the figures of Hepburn and Brazzi.*

Katharine Hepburn in SUMMER MADNESS.

all been replaced by the younger generation. Without caring about money, clothes, and means of transport they have either travelled their way leisurely around Europe living with lovers and strangers, or have worked for social and political causes bringing them into contact with the opposite sex and providing natural means of temporary or lasting relationships, unencumbered by any prejudice or puritanism about the clash of cultures, or by fears of the destruction of new world innocence by old world cynicism and corruption. But at the time Katharine Hepburn, as Jane Hudson, finds herself in Venice, she is in advance of the great army of tourists, reinforced by the jet airplane, the credit card, the cine-camera and the hired car companies, soon to overrun Europe. And to the movie audiences of the world at the time of the film's release it was the beginning of the wide-screen, deep focus colour and stereophonic sound era—technical innovations that had sent film-makers hurrying to strange places to film stories chosen for their scenic backgrounds. This in turn added to tourist travel, as audiences saw the sights of the world spread before them in colour and CinemaScope. This automatically brought about the end of wildly improbable romances as more moviegoers travelled as a result of seeing such

Renato is left on the station with an abandoned farewell gift.

films, only to find a good deal of disillusionment in the hard reality of life abroad.

Summer Madness however, was not filmed in CinemaScope, nor did Lean exploit Venice's crumbling beauty purely for travelogue contentment. Like a great artist painting a landscape, he has evoked Jane's first excitement with the pleasure and pulse of Venetian life, the great fluttering of the pigeons in St. Mark's Square, the rhythm of the gondoliers on the canals, the feeling of discovery and awe on finding so much to see and visit, the gaiety of the restaurants; and then, with the setting of the sun, the first loneliness of the evening, the passing of a young couple, hand in hand and in love, the soft laughter of intimate friends, the gondolas passing quietly along the canals, a song filling the air, the splash of a stone in the water, the sudden darkness and silence of a hotel room. Through a haze of summer warmth and evening enchantment, we feel every changing emotion experienced by Miss Hudson, as she explores, photographs with her cine-camera, talks to her urchin companion, and finally meets and loves the antique dealer. She is disillusioned to find him married with several children. Culture and temperaments being different for both of them, she ends her brief encounter. She leaves Venice in an affecting farewell waving from the train in one of Lean's many masterful sequences, with the station slowly disappearing from view. The sense of the city in its bewildering and beautiful ways and the fascination of Katharine Hepburn's performance lift this film above conventional romanticism. There is little surface activity, but its implications and emotional truths are deep and lasting. Its greatest strength is Miss Hepburn, who with grace, directness of manner and vitality, suggests that intelligence, self-sufficiency and a brisk, proud personality, can be as great an obstacle to finding happiness with a man as being plain, shy and ordinary, as was Shirley Booth who played the part on the stage. The whole has the intensity and control of *Brief Encounter*. In ten years Lean has moved from the streets and railway platforms of Milford Junction to the colour and splendours of Venice. The detail and the atmosphere are the same, finely observed, tellingly conveyed, and symbolically expressed. When the serenity of a canal scene is broken by a woman throwing a pail of dirty water into the water, we understand that daily life for the ordinary man and woman in both countries is different only in place, language and temperament.

12. The Bridge on the River Kwai (1957)

Director: David Lean. *Screenplay:* Pierre Boulle, from his novel. *Photography:* Jack Hildyard (CinemaScope, Eastmancolor). *Editor:* Peter Taylor. *Art Direction:* Donald M. Ashton. *Sound:* John Cox and John Mitchell. *Music:* Malcolm Arnold. *Producer:* Sam Spiegel. *Production:* Horizon Pictures (GB). *Release:* Columbia. Previewed in Hollywood. October 31, 1957. 14,506 ft. 161 minutes.

CAST

Shears	William Holden
Col. Nicholson	Alec Guinness
Major Warden	Jack Hawkins
Colonel Saito	Sessue Hayakawa
Major Clipton	James Donald
Lieutenant Joyce	Geoffrey Horne
Colonel Green	Andre Morell
Captain Reeves	Peter Williams
Major Hughes	John Boxer
Grogan	Percy Herbert
Baker	Harold Goodwin
Nurse	Ann Sears

Captain Kanematsu	Henry Okawa
Lieutenant Miura	K. Katsumoto
Yai	M. R. B. Chakrabandhu
Siamese Girls	Vilaiwan Seeboonreaung,
	Ngamta Suphaphongs,
	Javanart Punynchoti,
	Kannikar Dowklee

Story

In 1943, a battalion of British war prisoners in Siam, under the command of Colonel Nicholson, is employed by the Japanese on the "death railway." Specifically, its task is to build a bridge on the River Kwai, a vital link in Japanese military communications. When officers are ordered to work alongside the men, Nicholson, citing the Geneva convention, refuses to allow them to do so as a matter of class and principle. He is subjected by Colonel Saito, the Japanese commandant, to brutal imprisonment in the punishment hut. Nicholson stands firm and wins a moral triumph. He then takes charge of the building operations, determined to restore his

Colonel Saito (Sessue Hayakawa) addresses Colonel Nicholson (Alec Guinness) and the assembled British POW's.

Saito strikes Nicholson for defying his edicts.

Major Clipton (James Donald) visits
Colonel Nicholson in the punishment hut.

men's morale and to demonstrate to the Japanese the invincibility of the British soldier. The bridge, as he sees it, will be a symbol of British achievement, and in driving his men ruthlessly he wholly loses sight of the fact that he is now aiding the enemy. Meanwhile, a small British commando unit, led by Major Warden and joined by Shears, an American sailor who had previously escaped from the camp, is trekking through the jungle. Their mission is the destruction of the Kwai bridge, over which a train of Japanese troop reinforcements is expected to run the moment the bridge is open. Nicholson, who has just nailed up a plaque commemorating his soldiers' brilliant work, notices the explosives placed by the commandoes and alerts the Japanese commandant. In the fight that follows, all are killed, and Nicholson accidentally falls on the plunger, blowing up his beloved bridge, destroying it and the trainload of Japanese soldiers. The final comment comes from the British medical officer, a horrified onlooker, who shouts, "Madness! Madness!"

David Lean

"Where to film this story was our main problem. What place in those far-off jungles of Malaya, Siam or Burma territory, where the Death Railway was actually built, was the least difficult when it came to bringing in crew, cast, cameras, equipment, generators, actors, explosives? With Sam Spiegel and Jack Hildyard, we travelled thousands of miles just looking. The Siam-Burma border was inaccessible. There were no roads, no ways to carry in the equipment. The River Kwai actually runs there but it was very small. In Malaya we found a suitable river, but it flowed in an area of steady guerrilla warfare. Finally, we went to Ceylon. Some of the men we employed there had actually been in the war in Burma and Siam. There has been a lot of argument about the film's attitude toward war. I think it is a painfully eloquent statement on the general folly and waste of war."

Comment

An early British wartime film about the codes and conduct of war, Michael Powell's *The Life and Death of Colonel Blimp* (made in 1943, one year after David Lean's Noël Coward film, *In Which We Serve*), argued that the Blimpish version of war as being a kind of sporting event in which certain standards of gentlemanly

*Saito and Nicholson hammer out new terms
over a meal, after the latter's release.*

rules and behaviour were observed in carrying out the destruction
of human lives, was entirely inappropriate. War, as the ultimate
obscenity of mankind, was not made any less so by being prolonged
by gentlemen officers with Kipling mentalities who believed that
if a battle was to commence at six o'clock, then you waited until
six instead of starting an hour earlier, catching the enemy by surprise, and defeating him. In 1971, we witnessed the ultimate irony
of war with the court martial of American soldiers fighting in the
Vietnam war for having shot a number of women and children and
old men in the village of My Lai. At the same time they were on
trial, American airmen were dropping enormous bombs, in non-
stop raids, indiscriminately on soldiers and civilians, fields and forests, homes and barracks, animal life and historic buildings. The
airmen were not court martialled. They were killing from a distance. The soldiers, taught to murder the enemy, and often murdered in turn by civilians, were on trial for their lives for having

Alec Guinness and Sessue Hayakawa in a scene from THE BRIDGE ON THE RIVER KWAI.

Sessue Hayakawa as the rigid camp commandant Colonel Saito.

taken life among one of the greatest blood baths in history. Yet in war today, what human life is sacrosanct? None, and it is a hypocrisy from Victorian days to pretend that it is.

The tragic irony and disturbing illogic of maintaining any kind of morality during the immorality of the slaughter and carnage which is war, are scathingly expressed in *The Bridge on the River Kwai*. Although it is concerned with the Second World War in which (unlike Vietnam) everyone at least knew why they were fighting and whom they were fighting, it confronts audiences used to the simplified expression of war in black and white issues of good versus evil, heroes versus villains, with a complicated set of characters with different values and standards of behaviour.

The key to the interlocking stories is provided by Colonel Nicholson, obsessed with a rigid observance of military rules and the Geneva Convention, of the British class system, possessed of an inbred racial arrogance, whose very stubbornness amounts to a form of courage. In his desire to instil into his men a sense of achievement, to raise their morale, to prove their British superiority, he drives them into the construction of a mighty, impressive bridge. In doing this he becomes, at times, as seemingly heartless as the Japanese colonel who is in turn driving Nicholson. The British colonel comes to learn that his Japanese captor, at first just an oriental savage in his eyes, also lives by a code of so-called honour and gentlemanly behaviour, responsible for his living and acting in the way he does. Oddly enough, the American, Shears, depicted as Americans often are under disciplined occasions as having no sense of duty to anyone except himself and wanting no part of any ideology or cause, comes to feel a sense of conscience and joins in the commando raid on the bridge. The other British officer, Major Warden, played by Jack Hawkins, represents the generation after Nicholson, the cold, calm, calculating enlisted soldier who weighs all the advantages, and is out to strike the enemy whenever possible, under any circumstances, even at the expense of his own men. Yet, while this may win the war, we find it hard to accept such a brutalised outlook as being part of our side, part of our attempt to defeat the enemy. Colonel Nicholson's perplexities tend to unsettle the mass audience who would prefer to see clean cut relationships and responsibilities, as in the case of Shears and Major Warden, whose roles could easily be the principal characters in any ordinary war film.

But the narrative contains other matters to engage the audience's attention, most urgently the destruction of the bridge, and this tends

*Shears (William Holden) and Major Warden (Jack Hawkins)
pause during their jungle trek towards the bridge.*

Shears points out their objective to an injured Major Warden.

to take one's mind away from the absorbing question of character and motive, attitude and behaviour, which Lean has thoughtfully brought out in the playing of Alec Guinness, William Holden, Sessue Hayakawa and Jack Hawkins. While the studies in character are being formed, Lean has also begun to create an unbearable suspense over the fate of the bridge. The audience has been told repeatedly of its strategic value to the Japanese, and how essential it is that it be destroyed. Yet here is the British colonel, who should be planning its destruction, now so in love with what his soldiers have constructed, that he takes a pride in seeing it being used by his enemies, and is working against its destruction. In the time honoured tradition of the movies, the excitement is provided by the slow, desperate progress of help, in the form of Shears and Warden with their commandos, who fully intend to destroy the bridge. Naturally, audiences want to see it destroyed as well. After all, whose side are we on? Is it wrong for us to want to see the bridge destroyed for our own cause, not to mention that great expectancy we now entertain at witnessing the sight of tremendous explosions and a train full of Japanese troops falling into the river?

This is where the film differs markedly from the book, from which it was taken, and is the cause of much of the criticism made of the film by intellectuals—although not by the public. In the book by Pierre Boulle, Colonel Nicholson's strange sense of idealism wins through to the detriment of his own country. The bridge is not blown up. Instead he and Shears (who is a British officer in the book) are destroyed by Major Warden, who hates war and man's stupidity. The difference between the ending in the book and the ending in the film is one of the most graphic illustrations of why movies are different from books, and how a visual art creates an entirely different set of reactions and emotions to those evoked by literature. The reader can accept the non-destruction of the bridge. He has certainly experienced suspense from the writing, but not in the same physical sense as the audience watching the film. The reader will accept in written words the psychological implications of what is Nicholson's victory, the Japanese crossing of the bridge. The cinema audience, however, would only experience a massive let-down in their expectancies, to be taken so far in the excitement of destruction, which is to them the victory (not Nicholson's success in not having the bridge blown) that to rob them of it by leaving the bridge intact would probably have caused a massive protest. Realising this, and understanding the different needs of drama on the screen as opposed to drama on the written page,

Pierre Boulle (who wrote the screenplay with the uncredited collaboration of Carl Foreman and Michael Wilson) changed the ending and attempted to achieve all his points of view and dramatic irony by having Nicholson, as he is dying from Warden's mortar fire, fall upon the plunger which detonates the explosions under the bridge. To most audiences, this seemed somewhat contrived and unlikely, but few of them worried about it in the holocaust which followed, a truly horrifying spectacle of a giant bridge falling and carrying the train and the Japanese soldiers with it. (No one appears to have written anything from the Japanese point of view. Would Japanese audiences have wanted the bridge to remain intact? Were they impervious to the dramatic expectations experienced by Western audiences because, after all, the victory would have been theirs had the bridge not gone down. Or did they feel the same destructive urge as Western audiences and delight in seeing the explosion?) The whole terrifying incident is then summed up by the camp's British medical officer, who has been sitting in the middle making loud comments on the futility of war, shouting "Madness! Madness!" which conveniently sums up the intention of both book and film on its comment on war. In retrospect, few people who saw the film clearly remember how the end came about.

Colonel Nicholson displays misguided pride upon completion of the bridge.

*In this production shot, Alec Guinness poses
in front of the completed bridge.*

Jack Hawkins as the calculating Major Warden.

Whatever the criticism at the time (along with *Lawrence of Arabia,* this is certainly the most controversial of Lean's films) there can be no denying the place of Colonel Nicholson in the cinema's gallery of unusual men, who touch greatness even if for the wrong reasons. Many people find themselves on his side, even if his ultimate acts did serve the enemy. We think this way because, in spite of the immorality of war, we still like to believe, even while participating in one, that courage and idealism, self-respect and pride will see us through rather than a submission to barbarism. This is why we can sympathise with Nicholson's love of peaceful construction in the shape of the bridge, rather than permitting his men to do nothing and disintegrate into an aimless group.

*William Holden plays Shears, an ex-camp prisoner
who returns to blow up the bridge.*

From the technical standpoint, David Lean's direction is absolutely superb, keeping every aspect of a complicated and profound human study in clear perspective. With this film he became fully and in every sense an international artist. He came into contact with producer Sam Spiegel, and the American element was introduced into the story with William Holden as Shears. Working in Ceylon he went into large scale dramatic effects and difficult location filming with complete success. The picture made Spiegel a millionaire, also William Holden, who had a percentage arrangement in the financing. It made Alec Guinness an international star, and brought David Lean into the small group of *élite* directors who

Colonel Saito ceremoniously opens the bridge
to the accompaniment of a rifle salute.

Full view of the magnificent and costly
bridge. (See Technical notes: next page).

*Climactic scene of destruction as the bridge is blown up,
and the train is poised to crash into the river below.*

could with the courage of their convictions work only on films
which appealed to them and on their own terms.

Technical notes: The picture brought back to Western audiences
the famous Japanese actor, Sessue Hayakawa, who had been a star
in American silent films. The picture was made entirely on location
in Ceylon. It took eight months to prepare and build the bridge.
Fifteen hundred giant trees were cut down, shaped into pillars, and
dragged by elephants to the building site, miles into the interior,
to create a structure larger than any in Ceylon (425 feet long and
90 feet high) at a cost of over $250,000, for the thirty-second scene
in which the bridge was blown up at the precise moment when
the railway engine pulling six coaches was crossing it. The train
had once belonged to an Indian maharajah, and was sixty-five years
old. Six CinemaScope cameras were used, operated by remote control, to photograph the explosion. Experts from Imperial Chemical
Industries in London were flown to the site to lay the explosives.
Filming began on October 1, 1956, ending in May 1957. The bridge
was destroyed on March 11, 1957.

A victorious Lawrence (Peter O'Toole), addresses his Arab troops from the roof of a sacked train.

13. Lawrence of Arabia (1962)

Director: David Lean. *Screenplay:* Robert Bolt. *Photography:* F. A. Young (70mm Panavision. Eastmancolor, print by Technicolor). *2nd Unit Photography:* Skeets Kelly, Nicolas Roeg, Peter Newbrook. *Editor:* Anne V. Coates. *Production design:* John Box. *Costumes:* Phyllis Dalton. *Art Direction:* John Stoll. *Sound recording:* Paddy Cunningham. *Sound editing:* Winston Ryder. *Production Manager:* John Palmer. *Location Manager:* Douglas Twiddy. *Casting Director:* Maude Spector. *Set Dresser:* Dario Simoni. *Wardrobe:* John Apperson. *Property Master:* Eddie Fowlie. *Camera Operator:* Ernest Day. *Assistant Director:* Roy Stevens. *2nd Unit Sequences directed by:* Andre Smagghe and Noel Howard. *Music:* Maurice Jarre. *Arrangements:* Gerard Schurmann. *Played by:* The London Philharmonic Orchestra conducted by Sir Adrian Boult. *Producer:* Sam Spiegel. *Production:* Horizon Pictures (GB). *Release:* Columbia. Odeon, Leicester Square, December 9, 1962. 24,975 ft. 222 minutes.

CAST

Lawrence	Peter O'Toole
Prince Feisal	Alec Guinness
Auda Abu Tayi	Anthony Quinn
General Allenby	Jack Hawkins
Turkish Bey	Jose Ferrer
Colonel Brighton	Anthony Quayle
Mr. Dryden	Claude Rains
Jackson Bentley	Arthur Kennedy
General Murray	Donald Wolfit
Sherif Ali Ibn el Kharish	Omar Sharif
Gasim	I. S. Johar
Majid	Gamil Ratib
Farraj	Michel Ray
Tafas	Zia Mohyeddin
Daud	John Dimech
Medical Officer	Howard Marion Crawford
Club Secretary	Jack Gwillim
RAMC Colonel	Hugh Miller

Story

The opening scene is a prologue depicting Lawrence's death in a motor cycle crash, followed by a memorial service at St. Paul's. Here an agile reporter asks questions about Lawrence, thus providing the framework for a giant flashback, in which Lawrence's story is told, concentrated into the period of the desert campaigns. In 1916, Lawrence is encountered as an untidy, disgruntled young lieutenant on the staff of British H.Q. in Cairo, wanting only to get away from his desk and out into the desert. This he achieves through Mr. Dryden, of the Arab Bureau, who arranges for him to be seconded for special duty, to make contact with Prince Feisal and check on the progress of the Arab Revolt. In the desert Lawrence's guide is shot down at a water-hole by Sherif Ali—an incident which introduces Lawrence simultaneously to the ferocity of tribal rivalries and to the man who will become his firmest ally in attempting to unify the Arabs. Feisal is philosophically resigned to the absorption of his guerrilla army into the regular British forces. A miracle is needed to sustain the independent spirit of the Arab revolt, and Lawrence provides it, crossing the Nefud Desert with Sherif Ali and a small force and capturing the Turkish port of Aqaba. To halt another tribal quarrel, Lawrence has to shoot down

Jack Hawkins plays General Allenby,
seen here at Lawrence's memorial service.

Mr. Dryden of the Arab Bureau, played by a suave Claude Rains.

one of his own men. His realisation that he enjoys the act of killing sends him back to Cairo in a mood of remorseful self-doubt. But General Allenby offers arms and money and Lawrence goes back to a period of triumphant guerrilla warfare, destroying trains, defeating the Turks, and is hero-worshipped by his own men as "El Aurens," and made a world hero through the dispatches of the American journalist, Jackson Bentley—based on the writings of Lowell Thomas. On a scouting expedition with Ali into the Turkish-held town of Deraa, Lawrence is picked up by the Turks and savagely beaten. The discovery that he is not invincible, that he could be broken by torture, persuades him that he should throw up his command. But Allenby, assisted by Lawrence's own sense of destiny, again sends him back to the desert. Lawrence's attack on a

Omar Sharif made his début in English speaking films as Sherif Ali Ibn el Kharish in LAWRENCE OF ARABIA.

A dramatic sequence with Peter O'Toole and Zia Mohyeddin as Tafas.

Lawrence is presented with traditional Arab costume
by Sherif Ali as a mark of acceptance.

Turkish column (which had earlier wiped out an Arab village) becomes a brutal massacre, which sickens him yet he finds he lacks the will to stop it. He leads his force into Damascus, sets up an Arab Council to run the city, and sees it collapse under the strain of tribal divisions. The British and the French play politics, General Allenby calmly awaits the disintegration of the United Arab Council and with it the collapse of Lawrence's dream. No longer able to unite the Arabs, Lawrence accepts the rank of colonel, thereby qualifying for a cabin of his own on a boat back to England. Allenby and Feisal are left to come to a settlement, which will sour Anglo-Arab relations for years to come.

David Lean

"Sam Spiegel and I felt that *Kwai* had revealed a certain pattern; it worked out a general theme by closely examining the situation of one man (the eccentric Colonel Nicholson) placed by his fate in an interesting and foreign locality. We were convinced that the pattern itself was artistically important and that we could now explore it more fully. Our first idea was to make a film of the life and death of Mahatma Gandhi. We approached this project cautiously, feeling there was perhaps something presumptuous in attempting to film, almost in his lifetime, the activities of a man believed by his own people and by others to have been a saint. It was actually with relief as well as disappointment that we abandoned the project. To dramatise we must simplify. To simplify we must leave something out. To decide what aspects of Gandhi's life and personality can be decently left out and which ones were retained was a responsibility we were not willing to accept.

"Sam Spiegel had first read T. E. Lawrence's own account of his Arabian adventure "Seven Pillars of Wisdom" some years before its general publication. Like many another, he had fallen under the fascination of its extraordinary author. And—like many other producers—had entertained the idea of making a film on the subject. Now the film rights to "Seven Pillars" became available. Spiegel acquired them and there in India, we decided that *Lawrence of Arabia* would be our next venture.

"To say that Lawrence was a complex character is to state the case mildly. There is enough action, enough psychological and thematic material in "Seven Pillars" for a dozen films with a dozen different points of view. On top of that Lawrence and his book have enjoyed, or endured, the comments and interpretations of some

Alec Guinness as Prince Feisal.

scores of historians, soldiers and journalists, often with an axe of their own to grind. We met and engaged playwright Robert Bolt to write the screenplay, and together we worked out our point of view upon the man and the theme to be drawn from his story."

Comment

The success of *The Bridge on the River Kwai* made everything possible for David Lean, and naturally enough, Sam Spiegel anxiously wanted to work again with a director who had brought him such fame and fortune. Yet so meticulous is Lean that five years passed between the showing of *Bridge* and the opening of *Lawrence of Arabia*. From the Second World War Lean now went back to the Great War. As with *Bridge,* but for different reasons, a storm of criticism greeted *Lawrence* purely on the grounds that it failed to present "a true picture" of the man, and left him very much the enigma we knew before. It was generally overlooked that almost no one still living could agree on what kind of man Lawrence was, and those who had written about him, taken with his own difficult

Auda Abu Tayi (Anthony Quinn) counsels Lawrence.

writings, only confused the picture of him still more. Lawrence
was an incredible figure of a man, no clearly defined hero, a man
who deliberately created a multitude of impressions about himself;
who saw himself as a saviour of a race of disunited people (who
had existed for centuries without him and would no doubt continue
to do so) yet a man who achieved incredible feats of daring and
courage, who was widely read, a clever scholar, perverse, moody
and it seemed, a man who had homosexual experiences. He loved
being a hero, he gloried in recognition, and when it was denied
him, he went into obscurity and changed his name. He was tormented by self-doubts, betrayed by his own people and those he
was working for. Like Nicholson, he was an idealist, and in the
end this blinded him to reality. Both were individualists trying to
work with or behind the forces of regulation and authority (the
army), seeking an independence that they hoped would contribute
to a change in the social and political climates of their time.

Working with Robert Bolt, a new writer from the theatre, David
Lean made a thought-provoking, often touching and terrifying
study of an eigmatic man, which dared to run (with intermission)

Peter O'Toole and Anthony Quinn during a desert sequence.

Lawrence causes consternation among the more conservative British officers on his return to Cairo: centre, Hawkins, O'Toole, Rains.

*Lean emphasises the landscape with silhouetted
camel riders: the entry to Feisal's camp.*

for almost four hours. In spite of this test of audience perseverance,
the picture remains an absorbing chronicle throughout, a stupen-
dous cinematic achievement, a continuous unfolding of appealing
and dramatic images that remain indelibly impressed in the memory. Working for over a year in the desert in Egypt and Arabia,
Lean conveyed the enormous fascination which the desert sands
exerted over Lawrence, and to a certain extent over Lean himself.
Once again, his superb and imaginative visual flair is apparent
throughout the picture, but certain scenes are outstanding: the
first sight of Sherif Ali, a black dot emerging from a mirage; the
British army headquarters in Cairo, the colonels walking in accompanied by a march on the soundtrack; Lawrence in his robes, play-
acting, discovered by Auda; the massacre of the Turks; the derail-
ment of trains; Lawrence walking along the top of the coaches like
a god; the first sight of a ship on the Suez; the final Arab assembly
in Damascus. The film is so massive and detailed it is a tribute to
Lean's strength of mind and body that he could pull off such an

Lawrence's guerrilla army pours merciless fire into an ambushed train . . .

. . . then charges down to ransack and loot.

Anthony Quinn laughingly sports a trophy of war from the train.

enormous undertaking with such success. The acting is a pleasure to watch, with Jack Hawkins again, this time as the assured politically astute General Allenby, and Claude Rains as Dryden of the Arab Bureau, being close to perfection. Alec Guinness is impeccable as King Feisal. Peter O'Toole as Lawrence is an unforgettable figure, an intelligent, understanding, painful, desperate man. The narrative is thoughtful and perceptive throughout, finely aware of native characteristics, of class distinction and racial snobbery, inventive and symbolic, barbed and provocative, politically aware and above these elements, as with all of Lean's films, a deeply humanistic statement. Any man who is able to become a leader of people and move them into striving toward better conditions, is exceptional whether his ambitions be noble or otherwise.

The setting that Lean has thoughtfully created and emphasised for Lawrence's deeds is so magnificent and noble that his very audacity at stepping somewhat hesitantly into the role of an epic and romantic leader is sanctioned by his awesome surroundings. Here, away from all procedures, laws, systems and restraint, it is possible for Lawrence to develop into a hero, and he does so, driving himself to the limits of his endurance, and thus becoming frighteningly aware of his extreme nature—embracing vanity, courage, savageness and fierce determination. What is made amply clear is that once again a man bred of insecurity will push himself to superhuman efforts in his passion to realise an obsessive ambition. Bolt and Lean have brought out with an almost overwhelming dramatic force the contradictory motives behind military heroism, and in doing so, have made a classic film.*

---

* When Columbia Pictures re-issued *Lawrence of Arabia,* in 1971, fifteen minutes were deleted, making the action confusing in several key sequences in the second half. During the *première* performance in 1962, David Lean took out twenty minutes at Columbia's request. In spite of these mutilations, the picture was tremendously successful financially. Because of this success, the distributors will maintain that the cutting did no harm. This is nonsense; but this has been the fate of so many masterpieces which did not fit the exhibitors' and distributors' ideas of a suitable running time for a certain number of showings a day. In this respect, the director can have no control once the picture is out of his hands. But Sam Spiegel, who does control the picture as producer, must have agreed to these regrettable alterations. We can only hope he retains the negative of the original print intact.

Lean's unit at work deep in the desert.

Production Notes

The first shooting site was Jebel Tubeiq, 250 miles east of Aqaba in a desolate area near the Saudi Arabian frontier, with the nearest water 150 miles away, and uninhabited since the Seventh century A.D., when a band of monks abandoned a monastery they had established there. Lean and Young found infinite pictorial challenge in Jebel Tubeiq, with its fields of brilliant red sand dunes reaching illimitably to the horizon. The company established its headquarters in Aqaba. The logistics of moving equipment and personnel there from London were extremely difficult. Once there, the crews, the actors, the Beduin who gathered, and the animals, had to be fed and watered, heavy machinery moved, roads built. The temperature rose to levels where the thermometers had to be cooled to prevent them from destroying themselves in recording it.

Because of their modernisation, the actual sites of Cairo, Damascus and Jerusalem could not be used. These scenes, and those of the assaults on the Hejaz Railway, were duplicated in Spain, mostly Seville. While some photography had been done at Aqaba, the Red Sea port (having been modernised) was totally reproduced on a Spanish site, as it appeared in 1916, with a Turkish army camp laid out behind it. The terrible "blood-bath" sequence was filmed in Morocco. All told, Lean spent almost two years at the various locations. He became so much a part of the desert that he came to understand fully the hold it had exercised over Lawrence. This is why the film itself expresses so remarkably the feelings of Lawrence and the spirit of that time.

Lean (foreground wearing white jacket), and Freddie Young (behind camera with hands on hips), filming a sequence with use of a reflector.

Technical Note

Lean used CinemaScope with *The Bridge on the River Kwai*, 70mm Panavision with *Lawrence of Arabia* and *Doctor Zhivago*. Jack Hildyard, who had photographed Lean's three previous pictures, was not available for *Lawrence*. Lean now made up a new group, Robert Bolt, writer; Freddie Young, photography; John Box, production design, Maurice Jarre, composer, all of whom worked on *Lawrence, Doctor Zhivago* and *Ryan's Daughter*.

David Lean

"People said to me after finishing *Lawrence*, 'Now why don't you make a small film in the studios?' I don't want to make small films in studios. I've got plenty of time for that in years to come. I shall do another couple of big ones, I mean God knows what they'll be, but I will, because I like it. I like going out to strange places. As a property man once said to me: 'You know, bloody millionaire stuff,' and it is."

14. Doctor Zhivago (1965)

Director: David Lean. *Screenplay:* Robert Bolt, from the novel by Boris Pasternak. *Photography:* F. A. Young. (70mm Panavision. Eastmancolor, print by Metrocolor.) *Camera Operator:* Ernest Day. *Production Supervisor:* John Palmer. *Production Managers:* Augustin Paster, Douglas Twiddy. *Assistant Directors:* Roy Stevens, Pedro Vidal. *Continuity:* Barbara Cole. *Sound Recording:* Paddy Cunningham. *Re-Recording:* Franklin Milton, William Steinkamp. *Production Design:* John Box. *Art Direction:* Terence Marsh. *Set Decorator:* Dario Simoni. *Special Effects:* Eddie Fowlie. *Costume Design:* Phyllis Dalton. *Editor:* Norman Savage. *Sound Editor:* Winston Ryder. *2nd Unit Director:* Roy Rossotti. *2nd Unit Photography:* Manuel Berenguer. *Music:* Maurice Jarre. *Producer:* Carlo Ponti. *Executive Producer:* Arvid L. Griffen. *Production:* Carlo Ponti/David Lean. *Release:* M-G-M. Loew's Capital Theatre, New York City. December 22, 1965. 17,396 ft. 193 minutes (plus overture and intermission).

CAST

Tonya	The Gromeko's daughter, later Yuri's wife	Geraldine Chaplin
Lara	Larissa Guishar, later Pasha's wife	Julie Christie
Pasha	Pavel Antipov, later General Strelnikov	Tom Courtenay
Yevgraf	General Zhivago, Yuri's half-brother	Alec Guinness
Anna	Anna Gromeko, Yuri's foster mother	Siobhan McKenna
Alexander	Alexander Gromeko, Yuri's foster father	Ralph Richardson
Yuri	Yuri Zhivago, medical student and poet	Omar Sharif
Komarovsky	An opportunist who survives all regimes	Rod Steiger
The Girl	Yevgraf thinks is daughter of Yuri and Lara	Rita Tushingham
Amelia	Amelia Guishar, mother of Lara	Adrienne Corri
Prof. Kurt	Yuri's medical teacher	Geoffrey Keen
Sasha	Son of Yuri and Tonya	Jeffrey Rockland
Katya	Daughter of Lara and Pasha	Lucy Westmore
Razin	Political Commissar of Forest Brotherhood	Noel Willman
Liberius	Military Chief of Forest Brotherhood	Gerard Tichy
Kostoyed	A Revolutionary Nihilist	Klaus Kinski
Petya	Stationmaster at Yuriatin	Jack MacGowran
Gentlewoman	Amelia's favored customer	Maria Martin
Yuri	At the age of 8	Tarek Sharif
Tonya	At the age of 7	Mercedes Ruiz
Colonel	In charge of replacements at the Front	Roger Maxwell
Major	Second in Command of replacements	Inigo Jackson
Captain	A victim of his gallantry	Virgilio Texeira
Bolshevik	A leader of the deserters at the Front	Bernard Kay

Old Soldier	Who is also headed for home	Eric Chitty
The Priest	Who officiates at funeral of Yuri's mother	Jose Nieto
Young Engineer	General Yevgraf's Assistant at Dam	Mark Eden
Mr. Sventytski	Host at the Christmas Party	Emilio Carrer
David	Young Dam Worker with The Girl	Gerhard Jersch
Comrade Yelkin	Local Delegate in the Gromeko Home	Wolf Frees
Comrade Kaprugina	Chairman of the Residents Committee	Gwen Nelson
Militiaman	On the Cattle Wagon	Jose Caffarel
Streetwalker	Whom Lara meets on way to Party	Brigitte Trace
Mrs. Sventytski	Hostess at the Christmas Party	Luana Alcaniz
Raddled Woman	Who tries to save a baby	Lili Murati
Raped Woman	Who directs the Partisans to the Front	Catherine Ellison
Demented Woman	Whom the Partisans encounter on the way	Maria Vico
Dragoon Colonel	Who restores order after the rioting	Dodo Assad Bahador
Political Officer	Among officers during rioting	Peter Madden

Story

The opening, as in *Lawrence of Arabia*, is a prologue which leads into a flashback; here, under the great arch of a hydro-electric dam walks a line of workers. One of them, a girl, is singled out by Yevgraf, the kindly commissar, who asks her if the book of poems he shows her stirs any memories. Thus the story begins, narrated by Yevgraf, in Czarist Moscow, with its restless anxieties of a dream of a new Russia. Yuri Zhivago, orphaned as a boy, is brought up in the family of Alexander Gromeko, whose daughter Tonya he later marries after qualifying as a doctor. During his years in Moscow as a student, Yuri several times comes across Lara, the beautiful daughter of a dressmaker, Amelia, most dramatically at a Christmas party where Lara shoots her mother's protector, Komarovsky, a political opportunist who has seduced her. Lara is

Tonya (Mercedes Ruiz), Alexander (Ralph Richardson), and Anna (Siobhan McKenna), welcome Yuri (Tarek Sharif) into the family.

Yuri (Omar Sharif) and his foster mother Anna (Siobhan McKenna).

Alec Guinness plays Yevgraf, Yuri's half-brother, seen here in his youth.

led away from the party by Pasha, a revolutionary idealist whom she later marries. Moscow is caught up in the Great War and Yuri works as a doctor at the front where he again meets Lara, now working as a nurse. Returning to Moscow, Yuri finds the city transformed by the revolution, his family's house requisitioned, and himself under suspicion for the poetry he has published. Yevgraf, his half-brother and a Bolshevik police commissar, urges Yuri to take his family away from Moscow to their country estate at Yuriatin in the Urals. Meanwhile, Pasha, now called Strelnikov, is waging a ruthless war against surviving White Army units. Discovering that Lara is living in a nearby town, Yuri visits her; they fall passionately in love, but as he is returning one day, he is captured by the Red Army partisans and forced into service as a doctor. Yuri deserts the unit and struggles back across the snow-bound steppes

Geraldine Chaplin as Tonya, Yuri's half-sister, and eventual wife.

until he reaches Lara's house. Here they spend their last days together. Meanwhile, Yuri's family has been deported to France. Komarovsky reappears to persuade Yuri to flee Russia, but Yuri refuses and is separated from Lara. Years later, still searching for Lara, Yuri dies on a Moscow street. Lara disappears into a labour camp, but their daughter lives on, to be found by Yevgraf.

David Lean

"Film, I think, is rather like a mosaic. You start at the top of the left hand corner with a small piece. You add another little bit, and another, and another, and if you can get each little bit a quarter of one per cent better than it might be if you only did it once, it'll have a tremendous effect on the whole, because a film

Geraldine Chaplin in the doorway of the Gromeko household.

is a series of little tiny pieces, and I try to make the tiny pieces as good as I can. I suppose it does seem sometimes over-meticulous. Maybe I am, I don't know. I take a long time making films, because I spend a lot of time on the script. I work with the writer; and in some of the movies I have made (not in this case) I have written quite a lot of it myself. Robert Bolt and I talked about *Zhivago* a great deal and he wrote it, and then what happens is that I sit down to my typewriter and I start at the beginning.* I put "Fade In, 1, long shot," and I make a complete blueprint. I sit at the typewriter and I try to imagine what the movie, the finished movie, is going to look like on the screen, with cuts and everything in it, everything. I do it as I hope I'll see it. Now, I have this with me on the set. I know it'll work, and then I get the actors and I run through the scene and I will maybe change a thing here or there. Very often I'm following the script, because I rarely find that you can do something better at the last minute. I know this is against a lot of the new school of film-making, but I personally am very wary of improvisation at the last minute. I mean, I could go on for hours improvising in a scene, you'd have a scene in a railway station or something like that, and you'd have mobs of extras there, and you think, I can make quite an interesting semi-documentary sequence out of it, but it's going to get me away from the narrative, and if you are doing a film such as *Zhivago* where you have got an enormous amount to tell, in a very limited time, you've got to be very wary about going off on side tracks, however beautiful they may be.

"In the early stages, the director is, as it were, a shaper of the film, and then of course as the shooting gets nearer, he takes more and more responsibility. I mean he's responsible for casting, if he is powerful enough to have that control; that makes quite a lot of difference, whether one plays well-known stars or takes a risk with unknowns, as indeed we've done with *Zhivago*, in several cases. Then one comes to shoot it. I'd love to see the identical script shot by three directors. I think you'd find the finished results very different, because it's a matter of taste. I suppose most of my time I'm encouraging certain things and suppressing certain things in the people around me, in the photography, the sound perhaps, yes, quite a bit; and certainly in the actors. One tends to put one's own

---

* The Screenplay of *Doctor Zhivago* (by Robert Bolt, published by Random House) contains an enlightening introduction by the author on the problems of adapting a book to the screen.

Geraldine Chaplin and Omar Sharif in a scene from DR. ZHIVAGO.

Rod Steiger as Komarovsky, a political opportunist.

point of view over through the actors, and so a kind of personal taste, or touch if you like, will probably come out. I'm not quite sure. Above all, a director chooses what the audience sees and when. He decides whether you will see it in close-up, or long shot, on their backs, on their faces, whether it's dark, whether it's light, whether it's fast or slow, and that, in itself, has quite an effect, of course. This question of freedom, it's a question of one's record, I suppose, if a large company is going to put a vast amount of money into a film project, I suppose they naturally entrust that money to people who have proved things in the past, and I suppose I have had a fairly good record that way, I don't know, and I mean,

Komarovsky (Rod Steiger) seduces Lara, played by Julie Christie.

on this film, it's costing a fortune. It's the first time I've worked
with M-G-M and I've had no quarrels with them at all. They have
let me do just as I like. Fantastic freedom. For instance, we've got
two very rewarding parts for two women, and we've got Julie
Christie, who's not all that well-known and Geraldine Chaplin,
who's only done one film, and that's quite a gamble. They really
are big parts, and then we've got Omar Sharif playing the leading
role, and the first time he was on the Western screen, at any rate,
was in *Lawrence*."

Komarovsky takes Lara to a carriage after the seduction scene.

Comment

Thoroughly exhausted by the creation of *Lawrence* (the logistics of which, in the re-creation of his time, the battles, the people he knew, the places he visited, were staggering), David Lean took a long sea voyage and on the ship read Boris Pasternak's "Doctor Zhivago." The Italian producer, Carlo Ponti, had also read it. Both director and producer wanted to film it, and Ponti approached M-G-M. Had any other film-maker suggested the filming of what seemed to be an utterly unfilmable book, with an expensive subject matter, and no great public following, he would have been unceremoniously dismissed. But with the success of *Kwai* and *Lawrence*, whose grosses between them amounted to some fifty million dollars, M-G-M believed that Lean would make the book work as a film, and gave him the budget he needed. The result is a most remarkable and extraordinary film. The book, when first published after being smuggled out of Russia, received great critical acclaim.

*A tense looking Lara produces the gun with which
she attempts to kill Komarovsky.*

Mounted Cossacks charge a crowd of demonstrators.
An exceptional crowd scene on the complex Madrid set.

Its sales however, were not large compared to most books on the "best-selling" lists (which are turned into expensive films) and the reading public found "Doctor Zhivago" hard going. Like "War and Peace," it was seldom finished. The film, released three years after *Lawrence*, was received negatively by most critics.

But the public thought differently. With a magic that no one can ever explain, it caught their fancy and people everywhere poured in to see it. It became, together with *Gone with the Wind* (to which it bears certain superficial resemblances) M-G-M's greatest grossing picture (thirty million dollars). It has never gone out of release. Although often advertised as being "the farewell performance," *Doctor Zhivago* always returns and always has a huge audience. M-G-M, which is today a minor company in film production, with considerable financial difficulties, has lived off the receipts from *Doctor Zhivago*, and exhibitors who feel financially pinched know they can always be assured of a good week with *Doctor Zhivago*.

At the outbreak of revolution, Russian soldiers turn on their commanders.
Yuri and Lara together at the front.

A rare moment of happiness for Yuri and Lara.

Once again, David Lean's audacity arouses the deepest admiration. Here again is a subject of such sweep, power and complexity, that any ordinary director would be overwhelmed by it. David Lean however, invites, accepts and masters the challenges he sets for himself. Building an immense set in Madrid, covering a section of Moscow with streets, squares, shops, a tram line, with the buildings providing the interior scenes as well as exteriors, he went to work sympathetically re-creating the period of the Russian revolution with an immense amount of feeling and imagination. Working again with a large cast of well-known actors, he maintains the military theme from *Kwai* and *Lawrence*, but this time combines it with the individual passions of love and romance inherent in his earlier films.

Bolt's thoughtful screenplay works from two main points: the simple, heroic love story and the ironic social commentary on the cruelty and illogicality of revolutions. The cruelty of political idealism is coldly established. After the intermission, the two elements combine with the separate stories of Yuri and Lara into an engrossing drama with its tragic yet hopeful ending. To structure such a

*Yuri's half-brother, now a Bolshevik general,
warns him of the dangers of Moscow.*

complicated screenplay from a rambling novel is a literary achievement in itself, and recalls Lean's days with Dickens. Dickens and
the Russians have much in common, and *Zhivago* has elements of
Dickens in its family relationships, social issues, coincidences and
lost souls struggling with their destiny, their tormentors, and their
own consciences, and turning up in unlikely places. Like *Lawrence*
the story is told with Lean's favourite device, the flashback, as well
as by a narration (by Guinness) and with extraordinary visual
lyricism. Pasternak's "boundless, dazed and scented silence" of
landscape and steppes, snow and ice, desolation and loneliness are
captured with poignant sadness and stillness. The train again is a
symbol of meetings and farewells, the ending of lives. Unlike
Nicholson and Lawrence, Zhivago is not a strong man, and for the
most part of his life is wretched and ineffectual. He is a good man,
but weak and vulnerable, and unwittingly causes as much tragedy
as that committed deliberately by evil men, hence the remark by
the soldier "God rot good men." The fact that he is a poet some-
how emphasises his weakness, both morally and politically. Zhivago's appeal and his strength lies in his humanity, and his love

The train journey to Yuryatin. Starkly beautiful photography by Young.

for Lara while married to Tonya is not easy to accept, for the wife is not the conventional dull and plain housewife who has driven her husband to a younger and more vital woman. She is in fact as pretty and as interesting a woman as Lara, and Zhivago's neglect of her and infatuation with Lara does not make him an entirely sympathetic character. In spite of this, he is acted and presented with such humanity that few audiences fail to understand his emotions, his craving for Lara. It is this intense romanticism which gives the film its wide, popular and lasting appeal.

The entire film is not a plea for any one person. Just as *The Bridge on the River Kwai* saw a world in miniature bring about its total destruction, so *Doctor Zhivago* pulls back and looks at a teaming humanity in which the individual acts of many people have brought death and destruction to everyone. What the narrative seems to be saying is that no one is worth saving, all have gone wrong, everyone pays for the consequences. Except that in *Zhivago*, the scenes of the workers at the dam, and the discovery of Yuri's daughter, indicate that a better, if not a perfect, life did result from the agonies of those who died in the social upheaval. Dramatically,

Strelnikov, a fanatical Bolshevik idealist, played by Tom Courtenay.

the film is alive with movements, shadows and exploding passions, as Pasternak's characters come to life with amazing substance and persuasion. Memorable are the scenes of the beef-faced colonel being pulled from his horse, down into the mob of soldiers, and beaten to death; the train roaring past with Strelnikov standing on the platform; the charge across the ice; the shooting down of the white-clad boys in the field of yellow corn; the door of the train wagon being pulled open to show the death and desolation in the passing villages; the sweeping plains; the house of ice; the lonely countryside and the howling wolves; the forced gaiety of the last days of Czarist Moscow, all strengthened by the superb performances, sound effects and music.

When Zhivago sets out on his long walk through the freezing snow to find Lara, we are reminded of Lawrence and his long trek into the hot desert, the one to find the woman he loves, the other to find power and glory. The spirit of the novel is everywhere apparent, its elusive qualities and diverse characters brought together in an entrancing and poetic work, looking indeed, with its flowers, frost crystals, contrasts and colours, the visual and living embodiment of what poetry meant to Zhivago himself.

Production Notes

The cameras turned on December 28, 1964. Filming ended on October 7, 1965.

Filming in Madrid

"The Revolution simply provided a canvas against which is told a moving and highly personal love story. It was necessary to re-create sections of Moscow, since we were obviously barred from filming there"—DAVID LEAN

The planning and construction of the set took almost a year, the largest ever built for location filming, consisting of a half-mile long, concrete-paved business street dominated by the Kremlin; hundreds of shops, each a different enterprise with corresponding products on display, changed in details as the story's years advanced; a tram line and trolley cars; side street leading to a factory with smokestacks in the worker's section of town; the Red Square with a statue of Alexander II on horseback; a police station and a church; and three detailed interior sets with entranceways to six additional interiors. Door frames and window lettering were changed for the times between 1902 and 1935.

The Red Army charges from a snow covered forest. Filmed on location in Finland.

Another view of the huge set of Moscow built near Madrid.

An ethereal shot of the Red Army: footage shot in Finland.

Filming in Finland

"We shot in Finland despite temperatures of forty degrees below zero, since it best simulated the Russian steppes"—JOHN BOX, production designer

❊ ❊ ❊

Lean's crew stayed at Joensuu, 400 miles north of Helsinki, near the Arctic Circle and less than seventy-five miles from the Russian border. Principal shooting was done on the frozen, snow covered Lake Pyhaselka. Finnish Railways provided thirty-two railway cars and two wood-burning engines, re-made to simulate Russian trains of the early Twentieth century. The Lapland gypsies, wanderers of the country's remote northern section, became the film's vast army of Siberian refugees, perfect for Lean's needs, with the desolation of the land worn into their faces.

Yuri Zhivago as doctor to the partisans.

Omar Sharif on location in Finland.

Music in Lean's Films

The score for *Doctor Zhivago* became the most popular soundtrack album in the history of film music. In all his movies, from the very first picture with Noël Coward, David Lean has been well served by his composers in various ways and styles, and all have been distinguished artists in their own right. The documentary concept of *In Which We Serve* called only for the minimum amount of "action" and appropriate naval music, and this Noël Coward. wrote most effectively. *This Happy Breed* used so little music that no composer is credited; *Blithe Spirit* was beautifully scored in waltz-like, abstract strains by Richard Addinsell, famous for his "Warsaw Concerto"; the use of Rachmaninov in *Brief Encounter*, introduced as "on scene" music when Celia Johnson plays a recording of it, and then used as narrative accompaniment as she thinks back over her meeting with the doctor and her thoughts are heard as narration, was genuinely inspired and effective; Walter Goher with *Great Expectations*, Sir Arnold Bax with *Oliver Twist*, Addinsell again with *The Passionate Friends*, William Alwyn with *Madeleine*, and Malcolm Arnold with *The Sound Barrier* and *Hobson's Choice*, all wrote superb and skilful scores, being everything that film music should be in the dramatic accompaniment to Lean's visual mastery. With *Summer Madness*, Lean worked with his first European composer, the distinguished Italian musician, Alessandro Cigonini, who had scored films for De Sica. With *The Bridge on the River Kwai* he was back with Malcolm Arnold, whose arrangement of Colonel Bogey with his own march theme, became the first piece of music from a score for a Lean film to find a life in the world of popular music. By now, producers had learned the publicity value of a theme or song from a score being heard on the radio, and many of them deliberately forced songs and themes into a score in order to achieve this end. Lean has never permitted this.

For his next film, *Lawrence of Arabia*, David Lean met the distinguished French composer, Maurice Jarre, and his subsequent score for *Lawrence* was an amazing combination of scene-creation, atmosphere and drama. Jarre also wrote the music for *Doctor Zhivago*, and the great popularity of his themes heard away from the picture undoubtedly played a large part in making the film so popular with audiences. The score has been roundly criticised by music critics (who usually dislike film music of all kinds) because of the repetitious use of the two main themes. In this respect, neither Lean nor Maurice Jarre were happy with the result, which was forced on them by lack of time. Filming was completed on October 7, 1965. M-G-M wanted the film as its Christmas opening in New York, which left a mere eight weeks for editing, sound recording, mixing and scoring. Lean usually takes about six months or more to complete this important part of a film, particularly as editing means so much to him. Under the circumstances, a major score such as that required by Zhivago, would normally take several months to compose and record. In the eight weeks available to him, Jarre acquitted himself well with a haunting romantic score. It is tantalising to think of what a fascinating lengthy score he might have written had he been given the time. Lean's last picture, *Ryan's Daughter*, was also scored by Jarre, a beautiful piece of composition in all respects, tender, ruminating, romantic and sprightly, with a splendid march accompanying the arrival of the young British officer to the small Irish village.

Geraldine Chaplin demonstrates her musical prowess on the Madrid set.

David Lean comments on music for his films

"I can't read or write a note of music. But I know where and how it should be used in a film, and what it should express. I used to be very tentative about talking to a composer, but now I'm not. I think a composer must be told what to do. Very often the music supplies half the emotional and dramatic effect. Seeing a film before the music is added, an observer might think, 'Well, that shot's completely unnecessary.' But with the music he will see the reason for it. I think that to have the composer on the set before the film is finished is generally a waste of time. With Maurice Jarre I wait until I get a 'rough-cut.' Then I show it to him and discuss, very broadly, where music is probably to be used, and what it should do. He goes away and writes some main themes. He doesn't attempt to fit them to the picture at this stage. When I have the picture finished and edited, then he is given exact measurements, and he completes his score. Then we record. The first musical session is a bit of a nightmare, with up to one hundred musicians sitting there. Then we hear the score for the first time. Every now and again I'll ask him to make a slight adjustment. I'll say, 'This has an overall gay feeling to it. Can you put in a touch of sadness? Or can you make it more exciting. It's difficult to describe, but I know how I want the music to sound.'"

Tom Courtenay and Julie Christie in a tense moment from DOCTOR ZHIVAGO.

Interview with David Lean on the making of Doctor Zhivago

LEAN: Some interiors were filmed on the set. Where the view outside the window was valuable, in other words, the set of the Moscow street, we built the interior of the Zhivago house on the street, and made it a sort of studio and shot there. We did that when the whole family moved to the country, and they lived in the little cottage on their estate. The cottage was built in the middle of the fields and the scenes shot there. Other scenes we shot in the C.E.A. studios in Moscow.

The opening scene on the dam was fifty-fifty. We did the night scenes in the studio, because you couldn't see outside the window, and we did all the day scenes on the actual site of the dam. In fact, we rebuilt the set on the dam. The reason for that was it was very difficult to work in. It was a very small set, and there was the roar of machinery, water and goodness knows what, and the sound has suffered for it. If you have seen the picture, or you see it a second time, you'll notice that in the night scenes, the sound is better than in the day scenes. The reason is that we shot the day scenes in the real place.

PRATLEY: *One of the sets which fascinated me was the shop where Julie Christie's mother, or guardian, was working, especially at the time when the Doctor arrives when she's very ill. There's a marvellous scene where the camera moves all the way from one room, along past a glass partition and round almost to the front, and then you look through into another room. This is when he first sees Lara.*

LEAN: I'm glad you liked that. That was a bit of a cheat, actually. When the camera rushes through the house, as it were, from outside the windows, I was trying to give an atmosphere of panic, and so did this rather quick camera movement. That was in the studio, shooting on to the actual interior of the house, and then as the camera moves off the wall, we made a cut, and we did the rest of it on a set on the lot, at night, and I'm very pleased to say, you cannot see the cut. In fact, for the information of technicians, it was a ten-picture wipe, ten-frame wipe. The restaurant scene, where they were dancing and the procession went by outside, was done in the studio, and the shot of the singing was done outside.

PRATLEY: *The station scene was very much alive, with all the people waiting on the platform for the train to come in. Was that a real station?*

LEAN: That was a real station in Madrid, and we had a very short time there. This is one of the big main-line stations, and the Spaniards were very helpful in the co-operation they gave us. We started shooting at about ten minutes to twelve at night when the last train had left, because there used to be an absolute mass of trains leaving between nine and midnight. We started shooting then, and then we had to pack up again, of course, when the real business started at about five-thirty in the morning. We made the station into an absolute shambles. We strewed newspapers around the rails, it really made a real mess of the station. Then there was a terrible rush when we'd finished shooting to clear it all up, and make it respectable again for the railway company.

PRATLEY: What about the excellent train shot of Geraldine Chaplin arriving, coming back home?

LEAN: We did that in the same station, but during the daytime. We had real *wagon-lit* coaches, and polished them all up and made them look like a smart international train of that period.

PRATLEY: Now, in the train sequence where they take the journey into the country, this long journey, you had to do the interiors, I suppose, in mock-ups in the studio.

LEAN: That's right. This railway carriage, in which there were about fifty people, was terribly hot, it was in the middle of summer, and these poor wretches were wearing overcoats as if they were muffled up against the cold. The whole thing was on rockers so that we could simulate the motion of the train. To make things worse, when we do this, we have to put the camera on a separate piece of apparatus, because if the camera were on the actual train, it would not show the movement. It would be moving with the set, so we have the camera detached from the set in every shot, and working in those small confines, with the camera on a great big crane, with an arm poking it into the set, was pretty difficult. It took about two weeks to shoot the scene.

PRATLEY: This leads me to the sound. The sound in Zhivago is the most realistic I've heard in films for years. I can't remember another which was so absolutely right: all the train sounds, for example; this was true throughout the picture.

LEAN: Yes, I paid tremendous attention to the sound. It's one of the great technical weapons I have, and I think soundtracks are frightfully interesting. One of the sounds I was awfully pleased with, which the sound editors dug up, was the sound of the wolves. One day they said, "I think I've got a marvellous track, will you listen to it?" I did and I said, "Where on earth does that come from?" "They are real wolves in Canada."

PRATLEY: Do you actually record the sound of trains while you're shooting and use that? Or is it always different sound made up from other sources?

LEAN: There are vast libraries of soundtracks, but what most directors try to do is to shoot the sound when actually filming. I mean, if I'm on a train, and there seems to be a particularly good noise over a section of line, I say to the sound chap, "Look, have another run with this later, and try to get that, because it's rather good," or I'll get everybody to shut up, and we'll record a particularly good bit of bird noise, or something like that. Now, what we fail to get during the production, we hope to get immediately after the production. There are about two or three weeks in which the sound men are going around looking and trying to complete a list of sound tracks they've been given. If we fail to do that, then we call on the libraries. In fact, one of the trains, curiously enough, was a little bit of sound from one of the train shots out of *Brief Encounter*.

PRATLEY: The scene in which Strelnikov's train comes thundering by, the camera watching it as it goes past, was that the actual sound of that train or did you add additional sound?

LEAN: It was the actual sound of the train and we added, for about the two to three seconds of the actual passing, a little bit of heavy "clonk-clonk-clonk-clonk" on top of the actual train, as it gave that actual whoosh past. It was just added to slightly. That scene was exactly as written in the script, where you see the train rush past, and cutting to the close-up of a woman, she says "Yes, that's Strelnikov." I tell you all these sort of backstage stories, because everybody is inclined to go to the movies and say (I've heard them), "Oh, that's back projection, that's a trick shot, that's this, that's . . . " and so forth and so on, and they think they're being very clever, but making a film is, as it were, creating life sometimes by artificial means and that's part of the fascination of film. It pleases me to think, for instance, when Strelnikov's train passes, that an audience wouldn't be at all aware that we had just added

Geraldine Chaplin during a break in filming of DOCTOR ZHIVAGO.

that little tiny bit of soundtrack for those couple of seconds as the train whooshes by. You'd be surprised that the difference it makes to the impact of the picture. The audience, of course, aren't aware of it, but it has a great effect and it's rather like painting, in which viewers shouldn't be aware of the technique.

PRATLEY: And the scene where you slide the door of the wagon back to reveal the burning village and the inhabitants running from the soldiers?

LEAN: That was a set built by the art director, John Box. I think it's a *marvellous* set. That was in Spain, and we waited for snow, and we actually had the camera on a train, and slid the door open. That's as it was, it looked just like that, there's no trick in it at all.

PRATLEY: You mentioned the wolves and the sound. How did you manage to get the wolves there at the right time under the trees?

LEAN: That actually was done in Scandinavia. It's a case of waiting. You just wait and wait and wait. I didn't shoot it. It was done by a second unit. Where second unit work is required I do a diagram picture of what I want. That's actually two shots, one's a long shot, where the wolves are just little shapes, and the second shot, when he shoos them away, is a little bit closer.

PRATLEY: How did you manage to get the house they went to, surrounded by snow?

LEAN: That is another set, another marvellous set built by John Box, in the middle of agricultural land in a place called Soria, about 150 miles north of Madrid, and it's about 4,000 feet high. The set was built, and we waited for snow. As we started shooting round about Christmas, we had to start with the winter scenes. We also planted all the flowers, the daffodils. We got the bulbs from Holland because they don't know daffodils in Spain, I don't know why, but they don't, and we planted the bulbs in the garden there, and when they came up, we shot.

PRATLEY: How did you manage to establish and maintain throughout such a long period of shooting the excellence of the photography, the way it all matched together? I notice (I don't know whether you did this deliberately or not) that in the prologue and the epilogue on the dam, the photography and the colour seemed to me to be rather flat, but the minute you moved from the opening into the funeral sequence, it was different, even the lighting of the clothing, under the boy's hat, and in the trees and in that entire graveyard

*sequence, and this you preserved all the way through to the end
until you went back into the dam sequence again.*

LEAN: We did it on purpose, really, because that's a prologue and
an epilogue, and we wanted to make a slight difference, so that it
became like the jacket of the book. After comes the real thing;
the cut back into the main body of the story is that great big long
shot of the mountains and the funeral, and I wanted that to have
an impact. If you have anything very startling before it, it won't
have an impact, and so we kept it all very, very simple and very,
very down, so that when the story proper started, it really came
in with a bang. I don't want people to remark on it, but they are
aware of it sub-consciously, I think. I'm glad you asked me that
question, because it shows that it had its effect on you. The terrible thing with colour photography is it's much truer than people
believe. Let's take a very simple thing, I mean if you go out into
a park now, and we look at that park, your eyes are partly dazzled
by the brightness of the sky, and although you are not focussed
on the sky, it's flooding in to the top of your eye, and other lights
and colours are flooding in from left and right of you. Now, if you
look through a camera viewfinder, or even if you make a hole
through your hand and make your hand into a little telescope, a
funnel, and you isolate something, like a packet of cigarettes on a
table, and you take your hand away and put it back again, the
cigarette packet will become brighter, as you isolate it, because you
are not getting the glare in from left and right and above; and so
because in movies, in a photograph, you haven't got this glare coming in at you, it appears to be exaggerating the colour. In order to
try and cope with that, we keep trying to pull colour down. We
tried to do our best to keep the colour down in this. We used to
have a grey spray gun and spray certain bright colours with a grey
paint, so that they went down more, but still when I go into the
theatre, I think I could have sprayed it double the amount.

PRATLEY: *The other important aspect of the film is the acting.
I wonder if you could describe your approach to the casting of it,
and the playing of the parts? I feel that everything pictorial and
geographic is tremendously Russian, even though you didn't photograph it in Russia; but what did you decide to do with the principal
parts, when most of your actors are British? How did you go about
trying to convince us that they were Russian? Or did you?*

LEAN: That's fairly simple. As soon as we get the hair styles right,
as soon as we get the clothes right, and the surroundings right, they

Omar Sharif, sporting five weeks growth of beard,
seen with his wife, Egyptian actress Faten Hamama.

become Russian. I think, in fact, if we dressed Canadians up in German military uniforms, at a first glance, you'd never dream that they weren't Germans. In other words, I think our faces, unless one is talking about actual Orientals, I think our faces are more the same than we suppose them to be, and when we say "Oh, there's an American or there's a Frenchman" or whatever it is, it is likely as not it is because of his hair, his tie, his shoes, his clothes certainly in the case of women, and that sort of thing. Our faces are not that different, so I don't think it's as difficult as you think.

PRATLEY: But then what happens when they start to speak and accents begin to play their part?

LEAN: It's convention. Obviously they should all be speaking Russian, but as nobody would understand Russian, we would have to use subtitles, which we cannot do for a film of this nature. So that's no good. The film-maker must decide what he's going to do about this. What I did, for better or worse, was to have the well-educated people speak educated English and, because it's a vast country, we'll imagine that other people have other accents as they do in England, which is a very small country, and we'll feel they come from the provinces, or somebody speaks in this way and somebody speaks in that way, and we hope that that variation of accents would give an impression of a vast country with all sorts of people, types of people in it, which of course is true of Russia. With Omar Sharif, it worked all right, because he was supposed to come from the Urals, far away.

PRATLEY: In the train, the actor who was the rebel seemed to speak English in a very Russian way and for a moment it seemed to throw the others a little out of balance.

LEAN: He's a Polish actor, Klaus Kinski, and I at one time thought we ought to dub his voice with an English voice. It's a dreadful business, I hate doing it on the whole, but in the end I thought his voice had a certain strange appeal about it, which would be lost if we put a straight voice on it. So I left it. I thought, well, all right, the accent falls out of the rest of the film, but I'd rather have the general effect and a few people say "Well, I didn't like his accent," or whatever it was, or "It doesn't sound Russian or English or whatever it is," and have a few criticisms like that, than lose what I thought was good effect.

PRATLEY: Did you ever give any thought to having the cast try to speak with accented tones?

LEAN: Yes, I did. I mean some of them do, but it's just because they happen to speak with accented tones, but in fact it makes nonsense, if you're going to say they speak in English. I suppose if one's absolutely correct, one would say, as I said, that the well-educated people speak with a good English accent, and that the peasants talk in some sort of a Cockney, or some sort of country dialect. It might have been a good idea to speak foreign-accented English, I just don't know. One just has to go at it, and one may be wrong.

PRATLEY: *Several people have said they thought at times there were things missing in the film, and they assumed because they had heard you had to cut a lot out to bring it down to time that perhaps the narrative suffered as a result? The question most often asked me, for example, is why did Kamarovsky suddenly reappear?*

LEAN: Kamarovsky reappears because that is Pasternak's story. That is absolutely as it is in the novel. He's in the beginning of the novel, he drops right out of it, and then suddenly up he comes at the end, in a most dramatic way, and we kept to this and hoped it would be dramatic. People who criticise that had better criticise the novel! If we'd departed from the novel, I'm sure they'd have criticised us on that score, too! There are not great lumps of film cut out. As a matter of fact, after the *première* in New York, I cut out four minutes, and if you ask me what I cut out, I find it hard to tell you, because there are two seconds here, ten seconds here, little quickens up all over the place which I thought, having seen it with an audience, they've got it, and I'll jump quickly on to the next scene. That's all it was. We naturally cut masses out of the book; I suppose it would be a fifteen hour film if we filmed the entire volume. If we make good cuts, nobody should be able to tell. In fact, I remember a wonderful story about an American editor who came over to London years ago, and the director was very upset about this American editor's arrival, because he'd heard how ruthless he was. The editor saw the film, with the director, and he said "I'd like to take half an hour out," and the director almost fainted with shock. And he started to be very quarrelsome with him. The editor said "Look, Mr. So-and-So, I'll tell you what I'll do, let me take half an hour out and I will pay you ten shillings for every cut you know I have made." He took the half hour out, the editor only had to pay this man ten shillings. He was only aware of one cut! All the rest were little tiny snips, getting people upstairs a little bit quicker, through doors quicker and so forth.

PRATLEY: Very few critics seemed to have liked Doctor Zhivago. *What are your reactions and feelings when you read their reviews?*

LEAN: The power of the printed word is tremendous. When a director reads "take it away,—it's rubbish," or words to that effect, it comes as a shock and he's terribly disappointed; but then after a few hours, one recovers from it. In this case, it was rather different. I'd seen the film in New York and the two opening reviews were absolutely appalling, but the interesting thing was it went down terribly well with the audience, and then more reviews came out, and it almost looked as though these critics were talking about two different films. Either they were very much for it, or bitterly against it, and so I was half-prepared for the same thing in London, and exactly the same thing happened. We had a wonderful *première* audience, I think one of the best we've had, in fact, you could have heard a pin drop, and people were fascinated by the film and all sorts of people who don't know me came up and said "Well, I'm so enjoying it." But I was ready for the critics then.

PRATLEY: Were there any specific things which they said in their reviews which you felt were definitely unjust or unfair or even inaccurate?

LEAN: "Newsweek" criticised me, they criticised the whole film. In fact, it was a very angry review. It was rather as if a woman were writing about her husband who had just been unfaithful to her. They called it—I think the words were "pallid photography," but some bad word about the photography, and cheapjack sets. As a matter of fact, I know the photography's absolutely marvellous, and I know the sets are absolutely marvellous, and that rather comforted me for the rest of the review. Of course, the critics are difficult people to please. They see a film a day, sometimes two, and I suppose even three, don't they? Now I don't see how you can but be bored stiff—I mean, what can impress you after this diet? And I think they become very cynical. Here in London, the critic for a quality Sunday paper came in to the film something like half an hour after it had started, and he apparently came back three days later. He had plenty of time to write his review because it's a Sunday paper. He came back, three days later, I suppose, and saw the rest of it, but again I don't think it's anyway to see a film, and I've become a little bit cynical about them. To see the end of a film before you see the beginning, I don't think is the way to go about things. But it's a curious film—audiences love it. I mean, I've never made a film in which there's such concentration and silence. People really do seem to like it, but the critics—some of them—are violently against it. I've asked many people why it seems to make them so angry and I cannot get the answer. I suppose they dislike big pictures.

To be fair to them, if they see very glamorous photography, they may call that bad photography, they may call it old-fashioned photography, and that particular critic might prefer a film with sort of very downbeat photography, with no colour in it, or would probably prefer the whole picture in black-and-white. It's the same with the entire film. Nowadays I'm a little bit mystified, because when I go to the cinema, I like to have a story told to me, and I like to know where I am in the story. I like to understand it, and I've seen several films lately which have got some marvellous things in them, but personally I don't quite know what was going on on the screen at various key moments. I don't know if, for instance, a woman was supposed to be thinking what I was seeing on the screen, dreaming it, or whether it was in fact actually happening to her. Now, in my book that's not good film-making. I may be terribly wrong, but I like to tell a story plainly and as simply as possible.

In *Zhivago,* Guinness is the story teller. He's doing a commentary. We thought it would be rather good to have him actually saying the words. We actually did write dialogue for him, and record it, you can see his lips move. Instead of doing that, we thought it was much better if he were telling the story as if he remembered it, and intercutting it with the dialogue of the other people. I think it worked quite well.

Recorded for CBC
London and Madrid 1965–6

15. Ryan's Daughter (1970)

Director: David Lean. *Screenplay:* Robert Bolt. *Photography:* F. A. Young. (70mm Panavision. Eastmancolor, print by Metrocolor). *Editor:* Norman Savage. *Production Design:* Stephen Grimes. *Art Director:* Roy Walker. *Set Decorator:* Josie MacAvin. *Costumes:* Jocelyn Rickards. *2nd unit directors:* Roy Stevens (for the storm sequence), Charles Frend. *Assistant directors:* Pedro Vidal, Michael Stevenson. *2nd Unit Photography:* Denys Coop, Bob Huke. *Camera Operator:* Ernest Day. *Special Effects:* Robert MacDonald. *Sound Editing:* Ernie Grimsdale, Winston Ryder. *Sound Recording:* John Bramall. *Sound re-recording:* Gordon K. McCallum. *Music:* Maurice Jarre. *Producer:* Anthony Havelock-Allan. *Associate Producer:* Roy Stevens. *Production Manager:* Douglas Twiddy. *Production:* Far-away Productions. *Release:* M-G-M (UK: M-G-M-EMI), Empire, Leicester Square, London, December 9, 1970. 22,880 ft. 206 minutes.

CAST

Rosy Ryan	Sarah Miles
Charles Shaughnessy	Robert Mitchum
Father Collins	Trevor Howard

Randolph Doryan	Christopher Jones
Michael	John Mills
Tom Ryan	Leo McKern
Tim O'Leary	Barry Foster
McCardle	Archie O'Sullivan
Mrs. McCardle	Marie Kean
Moureen	Yvonne Crowley
Corporal	Barry Jackson
Driver	Douglas Sheldon
Paddy	Philip O'Flynn
Bernard	Ed O'Callaghan
Captain	Gerald Sim
Lanky Private	Des Keogh
O'Keefe	Niall Toibin
Moureen's Boy-friend	Donald Meligan
Constable O'Conner	Brian O'Higgins
Joseph	Niall O'Brien
Peter	Owen O'Sullivan
Sean	Emmet Bergin
Storekeeper	May Clusky
Old Woman	Annie Dalton
Policeman	Pat Layde

Story

Ireland, 1916. Rosy Ryan, a young girl of excitable and romantic temperament, is in love with Charles Shaughnessy, schoolmaster in the village of Kirrary and a man twice her age. When she declares her feelings to him one day, he admits his own love for her and proposes marriage. They spend a disappointing wedding night together, both unhappy in their inhibitions. For Rosy, this was not what she had been led to expect from the stories she had read of romance and passion. Father Collins, the local priest, detects Rosy's sadness and tells her she should be well satisfied with her life and such a good husband. A wounded British officer, Major Randolph Doryan, comes to take command of the army garrison nearby. Visiting the local pub—run by Rosy's father, Tom Ryan—he has a spasm of shell-shock. Rosy, alone with him, gives him comfort. For the first time, Rosy experiences the stirring emotions of passion. Soon they are lovers and the whole village knows of it when Michael, the deformed village idiot, finds a brass button of Doryan's in the cave where they have been, and parades with it up the street in

Sarah Miles plays Rosy Ryan in the starring role of RYAN'S DAUGHTER.

a parody of the Major. Meanwhile, Tim O'Leary, a Republican activist who has been searching the area to find a suitable beach for bringing ashore a promised arms shipment from Germany, enlists Ryan's help in salvaging the cargo, endangered by a fierce storm offshore. The entire village steals down to the beach to help with the operation, but on their way back Doryan's soldiers block their path and O'Leary is arrested. Ryan himself has informed the British, but suspicion naturally falls on Rosy, because of her liaison with Doryan. Charles, who has almost decided to leave her because of her infidelity, now comes to her side. But he cannot prevent the villagers from attacking the schoolhouse and stripping Rosy of her clothes and her hair. Only the arrival of Father Collins prevents further violence. Wandering the beach, Michael has collected the remains of the wrecked arms shipment and shows it to Doryan, who has learned that Rosy has returned to her husband. He waits until nightfall, and then blows himself up with the arms. Rosy and Charles learn of his death, and decide to leave Kirrary with at least

*Christopher Jones who plays Randolph Doryan
on the set of RYAN'S DAUGHTER.*

a pretence of mutual fidelity and the hope of a better life in the future.

David Lean

"Having filmed *Zhivago*, which was most difficult, adapting a big book which takes four days to read and would run for a day if we had filmed it all, and chopping it down to three hours, well, it can't entirely be Pasternak's *Zhivago*. And so Robert and I decided to do something in which we were absolutely free, from another author's material. We decided to write a story absolutely on our own, and cook it up from the start. We worked in Rome for about ten months. You see, I wouldn't dream of starting shooting

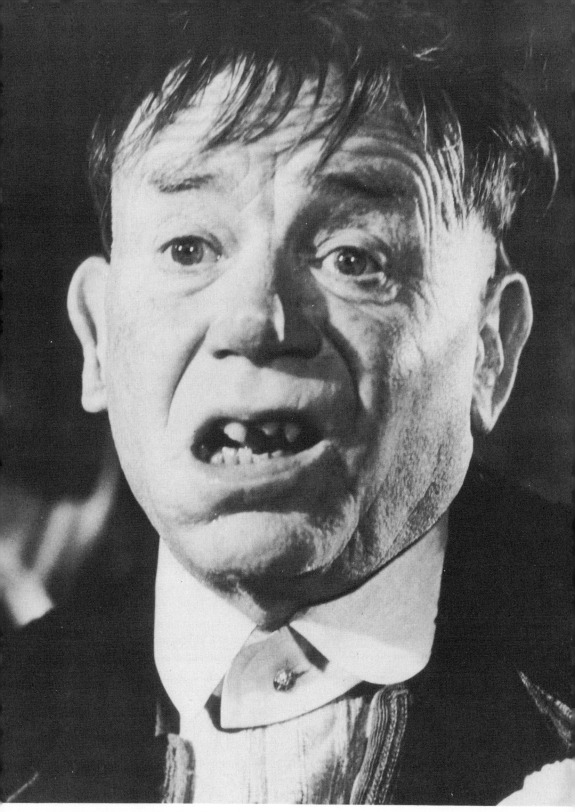

*Michael, the deformed village idiot (John Mills,
who won an Academy Award for this performance).*

a script until I was satisfied that it was the best we could do on paper. I would never like to go back to the script to re-write because it wasn't working out. Then it's up to me to put it on film. I don't want to put anything out that I could do better, within reason. Robert and I have some heated arguments, but by the time we've finished I don't think there are any scenes that either of us disagree with. The scene is arrived at by mutual discussion and I'd be very surprised if Robert said there was a scene he objected to from the writing point of view. As far as intention goes, we agree. *Ryan's Daughter* is about temptation, about a young girl who marries an older man and then has an affair with one closer to her own age. It's about the difficulty of growing up, the doors opening on adult life.

"Because the story is about the wild and rather darker parts of our natures, a lot to do with infidelity, I rather wanted to set it somewhere that wasn't specific. It happens to be in Ireland, but I think it could happen anywhere. We are dealing with the primitive emotions. You don't have to scratch very deep in any human being to get down to the animal. We pretend we don't but we do. It's very, very little way below the surface, the wild and darker side of our nature. I think the wildness of this country is rather good as a background for that sort of thing. I don't want an epic, and I don't want a 'little gem.' I want something that has size and that size must be emotional. When we are young, we expect there's going to be some wonderful something or the other in life ahead. We don't quite know what it is. This is what Rosy is after. She marries, it's a kind of disaster, and so she won't give up believing there's something better. There must be something more than this good dull husband. She meets this young man and finds this excitement. It's also her disaster. I think love's pretty fascinating, and I hope that when husbands and wives see this film, I hope the wife might perhaps think, 'Oh, . . . don't I know what that's like?' and not tell her husband so."

Comment

Lean, probably the most skilful film-maker in adapting novels to the screen, here turned to an original story with his writer, Robert Bolt. When the film was shown, most of the critics complained that it was a slight tale for so long a film. Slight? There is a wedding ceremony, a shell-shocked officer, a young girl's love affair, an informer at work, the landing of arms for the Irish revolution, a

Rosy encounters Father Collins (Trevor Howard) on the beach.

tremendous storm, a suicide and a number of other carefully observed events in the life of the village and of Rosy, a young girl who marries too soon and falls in love afterwards—too late. In new forms and settings and in other characters many of the themes and emotions, ideas and failings, common to individuals in Lean's previous pictures, are expressed anew in this beautiful, pastoral, gentle expression of an elusive passion. Self-destruction, inhibitions and idealism are all at work in strikingly different form from *Kwai*, *Lawrence* and *Zhivago*. The elements too, play a far greater part in the drama; the silent sands and snows and mysterious wastes of the two previous films are followed in *Ryan's Daughter* by the restless sea, symbolic of the emotions of Rosy, a girl of the village whose feelings and desires rise above her narrow upbringing and seek release in ways she does not fully understand, and in whose explanations by the local priest she can find no meaning.

The dangers of a woman's illicit love, so well conveyed by Lean in *Brief Encounter*, *Madeleine* and *The Passionate Friends*, is given a new dimension, a new excitement and sadness in this chronicle

Rosy meets and falls in love with Major Randolph Doryan.

of ultimately tragic events. This form of romance, usually contemptuously dismissed as "women's magazine" material, is hard to describe and hard to film without making it seem trite and sentimental. But such is Lean's skill at interpretation in visual terms, that audiences are never manipulated by sentimentality or melodrama. The sensual qualities which Lean conveys so imaginatively and effectively are found in the sequence on the beach, brilliantly edited, as the husband follows the footsteps of his wife and lover in the sand, and in the first scenes of love between Rosy and the officer in the depths of the woods. Again, Lean has evoked through Freddie Young the beautiful seascapes and cloud-filled skies of Ireland. The intensity of feeling in static scenes such as those showing the young officer in his quarters with his Captain and they discuss his battle experiences, the shell-shock scenes, the arrival of the officer at sunset, his death at sundown, the moments between Rosy and her husband in their cramped schoolhouse and home, are all further indications of Lean's understanding of what film is and how it should be used. Characters and atmosphere are cleverly

Rosy and Randolph ride into the woods, where they make love.
The two lovers enjoy a short but idyllic affair.

*Meeting for the last time, Rosy and Randolph
rush into each other's arms.*

created and sustained, drama is heightened, throughout the primitive, pastoral idiom of the film by the use of symbolism, bizarre and grotesque, but never to the extent that they are out of context with their surroundings or with the lives of the people.

It was a difficult film for Lean to make. As with *Doctor Zhivago's* Moscow, he built his Irish village of Kirrary at the tip of Dingle Peninsula, County Kerry. It looked so real that most people visiting thought it was an actual village. Once again, Lean needed all his courage and strength to see the film through. The weather was atrocious, with constant rain holding up the filming for weeks on end, with the unit and actors becoming bored in such a remote place. At one time, only a minute of film was shot in ten days. From a year in the burning sands of the Jordan desert, David Lean now went through a year of rain and dampness in Ireland. The result was worth every moment spent there, and how he sustained his creative energies and imagination over such an unusually long period, and how he managed to cope with and control his demanding form of film-making, is an achievement to admire greatly. And once again, although his actors will say that he doesn't appear to

Rosy's husband Charles Shaughnessy (Robert Mitchum) finally realises that his wife is unfaithful.

Rosy is hurried away from Randolph by her husband Charles.

A grim faced Father Collins (Trevor Howard) accompanies the villagers as they march on the schoolhouse.

concern himself as much with their work as he does with his setting of scenes and camera positions, the fact is that Lean has inspired them into giving remarkable performances: Sarah Miles, bright and restive, as Rosy, searchingly provocative, becoming aware through novels of her own sexuality; Robert Mitchum, never better as the quiet, diffident schoolmaster; Christopher Jones, so different from his previous roles as to be almost unrecognisable as the officer, and never as effective in subsequent films; John Mills, a Dickensian idiot, tormented by the villagers; Trevor Howard, forthright and fierce as the local priest, to whom all things are simple; Leo McKern, the blustering father-informer; a gallery of splendid players whose presence alone is commanding enough.

Together with the elements, the lashing storm, the shimmering sea, the rising wind, and the glimpses of personal pain and sadness caught up in the turbulent expression of the deep-seated Anglo-Irish hatreds of the time, this is not a slight tale running too long but a poignant love story carefully detailed, cleverly developed and sustained. Far from being a matter of scenery enveloping actors and narrative, the three unities of setting, character and events combine perfectly. The result is vivid and unforgettable.

A
GALLERY
OF
DAVID LEAN
PLAYERS

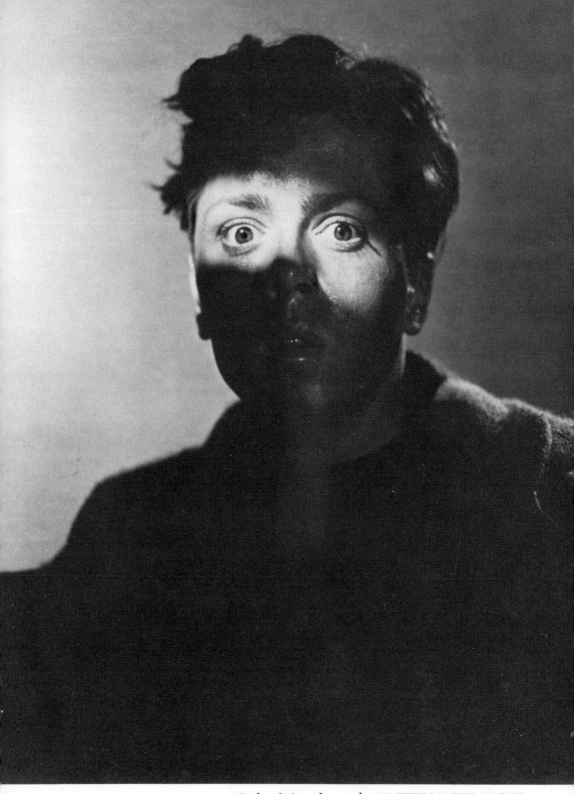

Richard Attenborough : *IN WHICH WE SERVE.*

Joyce Carey, who has appeared in many Lean films.

James Donald as he appeared in
THE BRIDGE ON THE RIVER KWAI.

Diana Dors from OLIVER TWIST.

Alec Guinness in THE BRIDGE ON THE RIVER KWAI.
Guinness as he appears in DOCTOR ZHIVAGO.

Alec Guinness as Fagin in OLIVER TWIST.

Kathleen Harrison who appeared in
IN WHICH WE SERVE *and* OLIVER TWIST.

Jack Hawkins in THE BRIDGE ON THE RIVER KWAI.

Trevor Howard in THE PASSIONATE FRIENDS.

Trevor Howard in BRIEF ENCOUNTER.

Stanley Holloway as he appears in BRIEF ENCOUNTER.

John Howard Davies who had the starring role in OLIVER TWIST.

Martita Hunt in GREAT EXPECTATIONS.

Celia Johnson as she appears in IN WHICH WE SERVE.

Celia Johnson from THIS HAPPY BREED.

Celia Johnson as Laura Jesson in BRIEF ENCOUNTER.

Gibb McLaughlin as Mr. Sowerberry in OLIVER TWIST.

Bernard Miles from IN WHICH WE SERVE (left), and as he appears in GREAT EXPECTATIONS.

John Mills from IN WHICH WE SERVE.

John Mills in HOBSON'S CHOICE.

John Mills and Kay Walsh in THIS HAPPY BREED.

John Mills in GREAT EXPECTATIONS.

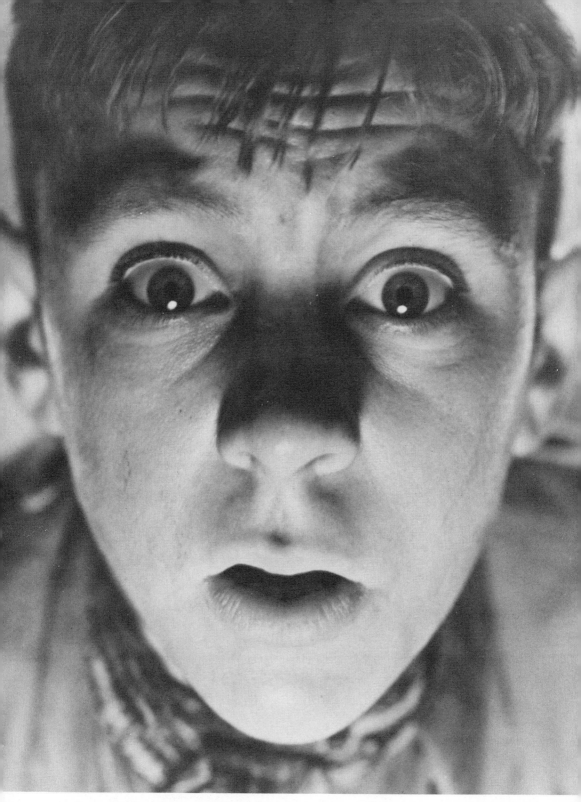

Anthony Newley as the Artful Dodger in OLIVER TWIST.

Robert Newton from OLIVER TWIST.

Robert Newton in THIS HAPPY BREED.

Claude Rains in THE PASSIONATE FRIENDS.

Claude Rains as he appears in LAWRENCE OF ARABIA.

Above and below: *Ralph Richardson in* THE SOUND BARRIER.

Ralph Richardson as Alexander Gromeko in DOCTOR ZHIVAGO.

Omar Sharif in the title role of DOCTOR ZHIVAGO.

Jean Simmons in GREAT EXPECTATIONS.

Francis L. Sullivan in OLIVER TWIST.

Francis L. Sullivan as he appears in GREAT EXPECTATIONS.

Ann Todd in THE PASSIONATE FRIENDS.

Ann Todd as she appears in THE PASSIONATE FRIENDS.

Ann Todd in the title role of MADELEINE.

Joseph Tomelty in THE SOUND BARRIER.

Kay Walsh in THIS HAPPY BREED.

Kay Walsh as she appears in OLIVER TWIST.

Conclusion

David Lean

"Where film-making is concerned all sorts of things have changed. Nowadays, as far as I can make out, it's not terribly fashionable to have good photography. People don't worry so much about having good sound, composition's out, everything's got to be rougher to look more real. I think that really makes directing easier, much too easy. And I don't quite understand some of these 'new' films. I rather like telling a story in pictures, but with many of the films I see today I don't understand what's going on up there on the screen, and they've lost me. I try to make my films clear, and this is not always easy. It is not difficult to be obscure and pass it off as being deep and profound. I worry about being old-fashioned, but I like a good, strong story. I like a beginning, a middle and an end. I find a lot of these new films are rather like diaries . . . 'I got up this morning with a headache, and my mother, who bores me, was making tea, and we sat down and had a dreary conversation about what she said to her aunt, and then I went to the office, where there were more dreary people,' and there's no end to it. There's no dramatic construction. I like to be touched and excited when I go to the movies.

"There's a tendency on the part of some critics to think that if a film is expensive, it's going to be an artistic failure. I think this is a very English point of view, which has spread to Europe and America. In England, money isn't spoken about, and if a man spends a lot of money or obviously has a lot of money, he's considered to be rather vulgar. This is exactly the same thing that happens with a movie. If a picture has cost a lot of money, and I wish to goodness the companies would shut up about it . . . you know, cast of thousands, millions of dollars . . . the critics have their knives out automatically, and their first paragraph contains the reported cost of the film. You're a great big elephant waiting to be shot at! I know the English critics are highly suspicious of anything that costs a lot of money. At the same time a non-professional who saves his pocket money, buys a lot of junk film and puts it together to make a film over three years on weekends, and the result is appalling, will probably get good notices. I'm not saying that beginners should not be encouraged, but too often, they are praised for the conditions they worked under rather than for what they achieved. I don't think very much of the opinions of most critics, yet when they have been unkind about my work it makes me miserable simply because of the power of print. It is there in black-and-white, while a remark over a coffee table one evening when somebody says, 'Oh, that's a bad film,' doesn't have the same effect at all.

"If I had been brought up at a time before the advent of the cinema, I think probably I would be a complete dud. I just love photographs; I love the camera. I want to go and look through it, in fact I looked through it yesterday. I'm very attracted by lights, by film. I even like the feel of film. I don't know what I would have done. Although I know nothing about music, I would love to have been a conductor. A painter? No. I haven't got that sort of talent, but I've tried quite often, secretly sitting down with a piece of paper and trying to draw a composition. Hopeless! I can compose for the camera, film is my medium.

"I very rarely see my earlier films. Old films, I suppose, are rather like a love affair, aren't they. I mean who wants to visit their old wives? However, I like doing films about women. I like telling love stories. I'd love to write original stories, but I haven't the skill. Every now and again I get an idea, but it's difficult to write it out. *Lawrence* was pretty well original. Anybody faced with 'Seven Pillars of Wisdom' would find it difficult to film, I think, so Bolt's screenplay is original in that way, and in a similar way, I think that's true of *Doctor Zhivago*."

★   ★   ★

David Lean is the only film-maker to have made three epic pictures in 70mm—long narrative poems of heroes and heroic deeds, of earthy passions and noble desires, conceived and realised in a lofty and imaginative style. What he has given the cinema in these and his other films is a richness of the human spirit and a concept of filmic creativity which is matchless and enduring. The times have passed which made possible the costly epic, and what Lean will do next remains uncertain. Hopefully, it will be a masterpiece out of this violent, strange and capricious age in which we live.

★   ★   ★

"I never get tired of seeing movies, or of making them."

DAVID LEAN, 1971

Index